Fairy Wisdom for Daily Life

FIRST PRINT EDITION, May 2023
FIRST EBOOK EDITION, September 2022

Typeset in Litania and Sabon.

The information contained in this book is not intended to serve as a replacement for professional medical advice. Any use of the information in this book is at the reader's discretion. The author and the publisher specifically disclaim any and all liability arising directly or indirectly from the use or application of any information contained in this book. A health care professional should be consulted regarding your specific situation.

ISBN: 978–1–7370545–9–7

Library of Congress Control Number requested.

Printed on acid-free paper supplied by a Forest Stewardship Council-certified provider. First published in the United States of America by Golden Dragonfly Press, 2023.

www.goldendragonflypress.com

Creative Self-Care through Fairy and Folk Tales

Francesca Aniballi, PhD

2023
GOLDEN DRAGONFLY PRESS
Amherst, Massachusetts

Contents

Introduction

The book you are holding in your hands is meant to be a companion on your journey to creative self-exploration through fairy and folk-tales where we can find nuggets of wisdom and psychological processes and stages, we all go through in life.

My intention is to provide a map or at least a practical resource that can help you chart your course with the help of fairy tales. While I am convinced of the value of this path, it is only one of the many available, and it will resonate with you if you are passionate or curious about folk and fairy tales and what they can tell us about our human journeys.

First of all, let me tell you a bit about myself so that you know about my relevant experiences and credentials. I am a creative practitioner and transformative arts facilitator and coach from Italy. I use creativity as a catalyst for positive change and inner development.

As a child and young woman, I travelled in imaginary dimensions as well as to other countries. I have been fascinated by stories and poems since the time when my grandmother told me some unique Italian fairy tales around the fire, while roasting chestnuts in the fireplace.

Later, I studied English, German, and Italian languages and literature at university. I then moved to Edinburgh, Scotland, where I taught Italian and studied anthropology. Scotland has had a huge impact on my soul; the land and its traditions and folklore have stayed with me over the years.

After a brief stint in Italy, I moved to Glasgow, where I pursued a PhD in Comparative Literature. When some years later, I moved back to Italy, I took up English teaching and undertook postgraduate studies in Expressive Arts therapies, counselling and creative coaching.

It was then that I resumed working with fairy and folk tales both in my teaching and creative facilitation practice, where I blend creative and expressive writing with other creative languages and activities: collage work, doodling, sketching, intuitive painting, free movement, sound and voice work, mask-making and dramatic monologue, ritual, guided journeys and visualisations.

As you are about to learn in the pages of this book, the fairy and folk tales I have chosen for exploration have been part of my existential journey. I unpack them here in the belief that they also may benefit you, as you walk your unique path.

I will not engage in academic discussions here, but I encourage you to look into Marie Louise von Franz's books, especially the first few chapters of *The Interpretation of Fairy Tales*, where she gives an overview of the historical development of fairy and folk tale studies.

Other important works belong to scholars such as Aarne Thompson, Max Lüthi, Maria Tatar, Joseph Campbell, Marina Warner, Cristina Bacchilega, Ruth Bottigheimer, and Jack Zipes. Each of these scholars (and others) has their own specific interpretative lenses; whether through literary studies, social history, myth studies, feminism, cultural studies, or folklore studies, they all look at different facets of the variegated phenomenon of fairy and folk tales.

In this book, I blend personal retellings of a few popular tales, analysis and insight, in the conviction that these practices are interconnected and yield good results for the story practitioner and lover.

I agree with Marie Louise von Franz that fairy tales are a sort of abstraction, the unchanging bones of a corpse brought back to life, whose flesh and clothes change as many times as the tales change sky. Thus, we can find many variations on a single story, depending on the various locations where it is told.

Marie Louise von Franz refers to popular folktales and fairy tales as abstractions because they get animated and revived in various guises at each retelling. The same is true, albeit to a lesser extent, about literary fairy tales, the written work of specific authors.

I retell both literary fairy-tales and popular folktales, as they have been handed down and edited—sometimes heavily, as in the case of the Brothers Grimm and their women "informants"—in written form. My method is informed by a literary perspective and an affinity for Jungian Depth Psychology. Specifically, we are going to journey through nine tales in search of motifs and themes that may be relevant to our ongoing quest for self-knowledge.

Each chapter includes a retelling, a section where we track themes and motifs, and creative process activities, whereby we engage in active imagination as well as reflection.

Active imagination is a creative process whereby a person works with their fantasies, dreams, and inner images by amplifying them through expressive languages such as the arts, movement, music, sound, dance, writing, and so on. Despite being credited with the first usage of active imagination, Carl Gustav Jung remarked that all of his patients engaged spontaneously in the process by themselves because of its natural healing function and characteristics.

In the following pages, you will find creative process activities inspired by the tales retold, inviting you to plunge deep into creative self-exploration.

The book is divided in three sections, each containing three fairy or folk tales that are considered as variations on specific themes. The first section focuses on the theme of 'Wounds'; the second is about 'Tests and Trials'; the third section is about 'Voices'. The ideal arc depicted in the sequence is from unconsciousness to consciousness, woundedness to healing (and/or vindication), tribulations to self-awareness and self-determination, self-effacement to self-expression.

I invite you to read the whole book first and then to go back and engage with the chapters and their activities in the given order. I designed the activities to amplify the themes of the tales and to allow for relevant, imaginative engagement. In other words, this is a book about taking care of yourself and your personal stories through the help of fairy and folk tales. It is about taking creative action, which is where all the gold is. Let us begin.

SECTION I
WOUNDS

Chapter One

The Wounded Seal

The first story I am retelling is a traditional folk tale from Northern Scotland and Orkney, an archipelago off the northern tip of Scotland. It was first collected by Thomas Knightley in 1882 in his *The Fairy Mythology*, and has been told countless times through the generations of storytellers. The title is *'The Wounded Seal'*. I researched and told it in the first storytelling summer school I joined, in Edinburgh, in August 2016. When I came across it, the story resonated with me because it set off a longing I didn't even know about. It moved me because it spoke to my need for homecoming to myself, after a long time when I had been projected outwards, and had not been listening to my sense of inner wounding. I had been dealing with a lot in my life, including a major operation, a sense of having lost a clearly defined vocation, a failed relationship, and adjusting to a country, my own, which I had lost contact with for a long time, because I had lived in Scotland for years.

Indeed, Scotland is one of the inner landscapes of my soul. There is something about the characteristics of the land and its people that I feel really attuned to. It still is, in many ways, an enchanted country. It is a land of stories, narrative and poetry, folktales and ballads, which is something that naturally arouses my devotion. I feel genuine awe when encountering a story well told.

A story is a key, it is a crucible, an alchemical vessel for transformation. Through its images and rhythms, it can stretch our imagination and the ability to explore our inner lives, if only we engage with it mindfully and let its resonances percolate into our daily lives.

Here and in some of the pages that will follow, I am giving my take on selected stories, with comments and creative activities to engage with them.

Below is my retelling of '*The Wounded Seal*'.

'*The Wounded Seal*'

A very long time ago, in a village perched on the high cliffs of an island in Orkney, there lived a man who was a seal hunter. Life was harsh and exposed to the elements out there. Wind and waves, rocks and thunder, tempest and loneliness shaped the character of the islanders. The seal hunter had been such all his life. His father and forefathers had handed down the trade, so that the seal hunter was only the last in line of a fate that had possessed all the men in his family. He was a solitary man. He traded seal skins in the market and made a decent living by doing so. However, he avoided human company and had never married. Other than the transactions in the market, he kept to himself.

One day, at the darkest hour before dawn, he set out in his boat and rowed off the rocky shore. Then, he put the oars inside the boat and waited quietly. It was not long before many seals swam all around the boat, playing and babbling like children. They seemed so happy and carefree. When the big grey seal flanked the drifting boat, the seal hunter stabbed him quickly, but before he managed to cast his net on the seal, it disappeared under the dark waters with the seal hunter's knife in its back. That night, the seal hunter only caught small fish. Then he went back home, sullen and gloomy. In the evening, while he was having dinner, somebody knocked on his door. The seal hunter was startled: nobody had ever knocked on his door, and his cottage was quite isolated and forlorn.

When he opened the door, there was a tall, dark-haired woman standing in front of him. He quickly assessed her. Her clothes were finely embroidered and rich, but her grey eyes were incredibly sad. The woman said: "There is a rich man who wants to buy many seal skins from you. Follow me, and I will lead you to him." Then, she nodded in the direction of a black stead. The man followed her without hesitation. They mounted the black horse and ran away like the wind. They galloped for a long while, till they came to the edge of a cliff.

Below, the green, foaming sea was raging and roaring. The man looked around... Nobody was there, so he asked: "Where is the man who wants to buy seal skins?"

The woman kept silent. Once they dismounted, she took the seal hunter's hand and ran towards the precipice. The man was astounded. The woman's strength was great. She was like a magnet and he could not stop. They jumped off the cliff.

His heart thumped in his chest, he was so scared and so exhilarated! The time it took for them to plunge into the green raging sea seemed endless to the seal hunter. He moved his legs spasmodically in the air, it all felt so weird, yet strangely peaceful. Was that to be his end?

When they dove into the waters, the impact was strong. It was so cold that it took its breath away, but as soon as they were deep underwater, the seal hunter was surprised to realise he could still breathe. Not only that, he saw that his body and his companions' had turned into seal bodies. They swam with ease in the depths of the North Sea, dark and pristine. It took a while for him to get used to the darkness. The water all around stuck to his new body like a glove.

When his sight had adjusted to the darkness, he started noticing things: the sea bottom was so different from what he had thought in his musings. There were sea caves everywhere and strange fish he had never seen before. The light of the sun did not come. He followed his seal companion when she swam into the opening of a dark cave. He soon realised they were in a seal compound. Seals were everywhere, in the halls and rocky chambers. They all stood still watching them with a sad gaze.

The seal hunter and the woman took on their human forms again. She grabbed a fishing knife and showed it to the seal hunter. "Is this yours?"—she asked.

"Yes, I lost it when I stabbed a large seal on its back"—said the seal hunter honestly.

"That seal is my father"—said the woman. "He's laying down, waiting to die. Only you can save him".

Then, she led the seal hunter along a long, dimly lit, winding corridor. At the end of it, they entered a chamber where on a huge slab of stone, there was the dying seal, panting heavily.

The woman told the seal hunter: "Come forward."

He advanced full of fear. He felt the sad eyes of all the seals on himself. He saw that the large seal had a long, deep wound on his back.

The woman said: "Now, put your hand on his wound."

The man was fearful, but complied. He put his hand on the wound, which felt cold, and then hot, in quick succession. The seal hunter was flooded with a surge of strong feelings from the dying seal. He had never experienced such a depth of misery and hopelessness, sadness and discomfort, in all his life. He felt the world was wrong, and things could not be made right again. He also saw his own life as he had lived it till that moment and he despaired. He was tempted to withdraw his hand, but the steady gaze of the woman and pressure of all the by-standing seals prevented him from doing so.

Then, gradually, the feelings of misery shifted, and he started to feel more and more peace, then hope, and great joy.

At the same time, the wound started to heal and, little by little, the large grey seal revived and was completely healed, as if it had never been wounded in the first place.

There was great joy and great merriment among the seal people, who danced for hours on end.

When dawn approached, the seal woman told the seal hunter: "Come, I will lead you home now, but you have to promise me that you will never hunt seals again."

The seal hunter had no clue about how he would make his living, but he knew beyond any doubt that he would never hunt seals again. He nodded. Then, he took her hand, and they swam on the surface of the sea again. Dawn was breaking in all its peace and glory. They rode the black horse to the seal hunter's cottage. When they dismounted, the seal woman looked into the seal hunter's eyes, took his hands in hers, and gave him a small sachet.

"This is for you," she whispered, and said softly: "Thank you."

Then she turned back, hopped on her black stead, and ran away as fast as the wind.

The seal hunter stood on the threshold, transfixed. For a few moments, he was unable to move or think. The wind blew fiercely, as is common in those islands. Yet, he was absorbed in all that he had experienced among the seal people.

Only after a while did he sense the velvety sachet in his palm and look at it. He closed the door and made his way to the fireplace, where he stirred the embers and rekindled a small fire. Then, he sat on a chair and looked at the sachet again. He opened it and poured its contents in his palm. He was amazed to see three little diamonds and a few rare pearls.

From that very day, the man changed his way of life, gave up seal hunting, and went down to the village more often. People took notice of his sudden change and, all in all, were happy to have him as their companion. The seal hunter turned into a fine craftsman. He set up a workshop and also hired a few fellow villagers. It was not long before he noticed a bonnie lass coming to his workshop...

Themes and Motifs

The first time I came across this tale, it resonated with me at an unfathomable level I could not fully comprehend. I was so struck that I decided to make it mine and retell it in my first storytelling performance. It only lasted a few minutes, but it was a powerful experience for me, the teller.

Somehow, I felt this story was about me and a wound in my feminine soul.

I think that different stories resonate with us at different times in our lives and that their significance for us may change depending on what is foregrounded in our lives at any given time. Thus, back in 2016, it was a time when I was reckoning with my professional identity and with my sensation of being stuck in my creative longings. Most of the time, I did not know how I could work with my frustration. I did know that creativity and story language were my irreplaceable medicines, my power practices.

'The Wounded Seal', like a lot of stories, can be read on many levels.

Here, I offer a foray into a few of its themes and symbols, being inspired by the idea that each single image, object, animal, character in a story can talk about us, once we take the time to consult it, like an oracle or a magical mirror. That is, once we attend to our own responses and intricate resonances with the tale.

I also believe serendipity exists and it is a key element in discovering new patterns and making new paths, forging new directions for ourselves and our lives.

'The Wounded Seal' starts in a desolate Northern village swept by the elements: wind and waters lick rocks and men into unique shapes.

Then, there is a lonely man trapped into an inherited fate: he has always been a seal hunter, like his father, his grandfather, and his great grand-father. His only way of relating to other human beings is through market transactions, selling and buying. Apart from that, he wants to be left alone and keeps to himself.

This is the condition of the ego when keeping us alive in automatic, default mode. The ego keeps us in what we have always known and experienced, in safe discomfort.

When seal hunting, out at sea, the man is quick and canny, yet he acts largely unaware, therefore, on that day, his prey escapes and he can only fare on small fish. That is, when we play safe, we obtain meagre results.

Then, something unexpected happens, in the form of an unknown woman knocking on his door. A call to adventure, or a call into the unknown.

At first, the woman allures the seal hunter with the bait of having him sell seal skins. This is the trick mystery plays on us to get us out of our dens. And the seal hunter—the ego—follows suit.

The woman (the soul) is sad, but she knows the cure and leads the seal hunter (the ego) into a literal and metaphorical descent into the depths of the unconscious (waters) where, by feeling another creature's pain, he faces his own woundedness too.

The alchemy of transformation happens when the wound is exposed and the seal hunter, who is both the wounding and the wounded in his own turn, ends up becoming the healer. There is much to be said about the need to have a healthy, integrated, wholesome ego to live with integrity and self-responsibility.

After experiencing all the range of feelings from despair to deep joy—the man (the ego) knows there is no going back: he chooses for the first time consciously and with full awareness in his life not to hurt seals again. A sort of ancestral curse is lifted: he is now free to choose his own destiny, despite (or because of) great uncertainty.

This tale speaks (and spoke) to me volumes because of its emphasis on the need to acknowledge our woundedness and connection to other living beings, to heal and be healed. The tale beautifully illustrates the concept of seamless interconnection across the whole spectrum of life. Moreover, it also is about our primal, inner wound, its acknowledgement and confrontation to heal and integrate the various parts and aspects of our psyche.

The soul calls us back home through our wounds. Both of us long for reunion; we can even pine for it, but when we do follow her promptings, we can become whole again. The seal hunter is honest in recognizing and admitting that the knife belongs to him. In other words, the first step towards recovery is honesty with self in recognizing our manipulations, projections, and instrumental reasoning to have an advantage over a projected enemy or prey.

We are the only ones who can heal ourselves, if we acknowledge our longing, if we allow for a reunion with our souls.

Our cravings come with all the symptoms of an addiction meant to dumb us down to soulless life conditions. And yet, soul is a quality of attention; and if we can shift our perception—which is Dion Fortune's definition of magic—we can change our life conditions—inside and outside—from soulless to soulful.

What is soulless?

It is automatic, unexamined living, it is going through the motions.

What is soulful?

It is living in and with attention. It is living with our most fundamental questions. It is attending to them and stretching to listen to the whispered answers or possibilities. Thus, we give ourselves permission to be in contact, attuned to our own souls, when we are mindful, when we stay and attend to all our emotions, without denying or suppressing them, but acknowledging their presence with compassion.

In *'The Wounded Seal'*, the other great presence is the elemental landscape made of rock, wind, and raging sea. To my mind, they do not only represent nature in the Orkney, but also embody a condition or a state of the mind, as well as stark elemental powers.

Rock is quintessentially a place where biological life cannot root. Yet, occasionally, a unique plant, tree, or flower germinates in its cracks. Wind and waters model and shape rocks into form over centuries and thousands of years. They are elemental forces. They represent those places of uncompromised, unredeemed power within us that are pristine, both generative and destructive, sometimes barren, often free and relentless at the same time. Their forlorn strength is both their power and their weakness—or wound.

In the beginning, the seal hunter is trapped in fateful ancestral patterns. His wound has to do with the relational patterns between the family or close community on one hand and the child/youth on the other. He continues to live in the way family and community expects him to. He has conformed to the way things have always been. As a consequence of not having discovered his deep self, the seal hunter lives on a surface level.

Only by following the mysterious, sad woman and taking the deep dive, literally and metaphorically, he is able to uncover his deep self. And then, he is capable of choice, commitment, and change. Compassion is the bridge to responsible freedom.

The gift he receives from the seal woman—diamonds and rare pearls—has more than literal import. The seal hunter, who has committed to change, even if uncertain about his future, receives precious gems that, no doubt, make implementing his choice easier. Nonetheless, it is only once he is committed, once he has pledged his heart and mind, that the unexpected gift comes.

The same holds true when we are committed to meaningful change in our lives. We may not see the whole path ahead, we may clear the path ourselves for a very long stretch, but unexpected gifts come our way, and if we are wise enough, we recognize them as such and as signs of confirmation on our paths.

About one year after coming across and performing this story in the summer school, I took up counselling and expressive arts therapies, as well as creative coaching. From August 2017 to December 2019, I underwent a deep experiential and intellectual training. Once I was committed, the gifts came in various forms, such as new friends, deep insights, invaluable learning, and powerful ways to experiment by myself and with the companions I met along the way. The pull of creativity and self-expression became stronger and stronger, as well as the call to facilitate others' expressive processes.

We come into this world wounded—through our ancestral lines and the symbiotic or detached relationship with our primary caregivers. It is part of our life tasks to heal that primal wound, to set our ancestors and ourselves free. When we heal the wound, we can go on engaging more meaningfully with other people and awaken more deeply inside ourselves.

The first step is to see and acknowledge our wounds and to be willing to do the inner work for healing and release. There are going to be other challenges if, and when, we resolve this one, but first things come first. One step at a time.

'The Wounded Seal' has also been adopted by groups wanting to discuss and instil in the youth the moral value of empathy and compassion and a sense of deep care for other than human creatures, such as wild animals and their environments.

It certainly is a relevant story to this end, since we cannot be awakened to outside nature without finding nature within us. I believe that *'The Wounded Seal'* can be put to good use if we read it as a tale elaborating on the primal wound humans experience and too often carry unhealed throughout their lives, thus inflicting pain to other creatures too.

The primal wound is profound by its very nature and can reach into the recesses of the individual and collective psyches, in the sense of "a world that cannot be made right again," unless the hand that wounds becomes the very hand that heals too.

In the healing act, the seal hunter not only bestows new life on the large grey seal, that unguarded innocence—notice that the seal hunter has stabbed the seal in its back—and playfulness that potentially is inside everyone, but also restores his own full humanity and creativity.

It is important that the seal hunter's hand wields both the fishing knife and deep healing power, a power the seal hunter does not know and is afraid of, because it takes him into unknown, painful depths of feeling. He deals with both the poison and the cure for the poison.

The same life-giving power is within us. It certainly takes honesty, courage, and humility, those qualities of openness that can lead us through our own regeneration process.

The seal woman tells the seal hunter that the large grey seal is her dying father. How beautiful that a father should be depicted as a large, playful seal, a depiction whose sense and meaning are missing from our societies' patriarchal values. It is beautiful and fitting that the father(s) of the soul should be innocence and playfulness, to be seen as pristine qualities of being, as inherent qualities in the ground of all being—Deity, God or Goddess—as embodiments of the profound creativity of life in the cosmos.

While destruction cannot be pre-empted all the time in the world, and often it can be regenerative, it seems to me that *'The Wounded Seal'* can resonate with those who have an inner sense of the divine as life itself, thus going beyond all notions of omnipotence, into an awareness of deity as accompanying earthly creatures, instead of shielding or punishing them. The sense of co-creation and cosmic companionship is one of the deep, hidden themes of *'The Wounded Seal'*.

Creative Process Activities

It is time to get our hands dirty and dive deep into the creative process. How can we work with *'The Wounded Seal'* and its images? First, I suggest you re-read the tale, and if you are curious, even look up Thomas Knightley's version on the web.

Activity n. 1

While reading, highlight or take note of all the scenes that take your imagination. Then, take out your favourite, easy art supplies. Make sure you gather the following basic "ingredients": magazines with a lot of pictures of people, places, animals and the like; glue, acrylic paints, gel pens, markers; a journal, a pen, a cardboard sheet, or other sturdy paper.

Keeping *'The Wounded Seal'* in mind, flip through your magazines and select images intuitively, without overthinking, then tear them; there is no need to use scissors. Gather all the torn images in one place, like a folder or a plastic bag. Then, shake them up, or mix them and take them out one by one, asking the following questions about each image:

What do I see that can help me relate to the story?
How do I feel when I look at it?
How does it relate to me or my current life situation?
What is its gift?

Journal about all of the questions, while observing one image at a time, keeping a soft focus and an open attitude. Write down all that comes, even the seemingly unrelated or irrelevant.

If you are tired or busy, you can leave the process at this time and get back to it a few hours later or in a day or two. When you get back, re-read the story, and then take out your cardboard base and glue.

Start selecting the images and paste them on the cardboard. Do take notice of your process. For example, are you starting from the centre or at the edges of the cardboard base?

Paste all the images one by one, conflating, mixing, and modifying them as you see fit. You will find new associations between the story, the images you work on, and your life at the moment.

Once you have finished, give a title to your work in your journal and explore its meaning and associations in writing. If you feel so inclined, observe your collage and use it as a springboard for an improvised story.

Remember to record your voice as you tell it. Your mobile phone, or other similar device, is all you need. You can repeat the storytelling process more than once by focusing on different elements or areas of your collage, then tell a framing story for them all.

Recording your stories is key, as it will preserve their improvised quality and will provide you with insights into each new listening.

Activity n. 2

An alternative activity is to storyboard *'The Wounded Seal'* by drawing and colouring the main scenes of the story in sequence. Then, select one or two scenes you want to focus on. Select them intuitively. Select those you are drawn to. Observe these scenes closely, and reconstruct them in your mind or on paper. Close your eyes and enter those scenes. Pretend to be there. Answer the following questions:

Who are you in the scene?
Where are you located in the scene?
Are you alone, or are there others? Who?
What are you learning and/or feeling?
How can you bring back this knowledge into the present moment?
What do you still need to find out?

After a while, open your eyes and report the answers in your journal. If you receive actionable insights, do act on them.

Chapter Two

Misfortune

The second tale in this book comes from Palermo, Sicily. The Italian writer Italo Calvino included it in its Italian Folktales (first published in Italian in 1956), a book which contains two hundred tales collected from the regional traditions of Italy. The tale has been translated into English under the title *'Misfortune'*.

Despite being an Italian folktale, I first came across it at an online storytelling event in English. It goes like this.

'Misfortune'

Long ago, the King of Spain was captured and dethroned by his enemies and his queen and seven daughters had to fend for themselves in the world. They had to leave the royal palace and live in a modest room, where they did housework for themselves and other families to earn their meagre living.

Times were hard; everywhere people were starving or barely surviving. The queen and her daughters were no exceptions.

One day, the queen went to the market to buy some food and was enticed by the look and texture of some figs. She decided to buy a few, just to be able to keep the memory of the good old times alive. As she paid for the figs, an old beggar came along asking for alms. The queen sighed and told the old woman she would have helped her if she hadn't been poor too.

The beggar inquired about the queen's plight, and thus the queen told her story.

"Alas—said the beggar—your condition will not improve unless you send away one of your daughters, for she really is ill-starred."

The queen was horrified at the thought of having to part with one of his daughters, and faltered; yet, she asked: "Who is my ill-starred daughter?"

"The one who sleeps with her arms crossed," the old woman said. "While they are sleeping, take a candle and check them out. You will find out who the ill-starred one is."

At midnight, the queen did as the old woman had advised. She lit a candle and reviewed the way her seven daughters slept, starting from the eldest. Each one slept in a different position and none had her arms crossed, so that by the sixth daughter, the queen started to sigh with relief; but when she approached her seventh daughter, who was also the youngest, the queen saw that she was sleeping with her arms crossed.

The queen broke into sobs and the youngest daughter woke up.

"What's the matter, mother? Why are you crying so much?"

The queen was full of despair and told her what she had learned from the beggar. "The one who sleeps with crossed arms happens to be you," the queen said, breaking into tears again.

The girl, who loved her mother dearly, said: "If I am the cause of such a great misfortune for you and my sisters, I will leave at once." She put on a brave face, made a little bundle of her few possessions, and left their humble place. The queen blessed her in tears.

The girl left the village behind and took a path through the forest. When she emerged from the forest, she came across a moor, where an isolated house stood. She took heart when she saw there was light inside. She knocked on the door. A young woman came to open it.

The young girl asked for alms and the woman invited her to go inside and gave her bread and water. Then she inquired about her.

"What's your name?"—the woman asked.

"Misfortune"—said the girl.

"Can you sweep the floor, do the dishes and the housework?"

"I certainly can"—answered the girl.

"Then,"—said the woman nodding to the other women in the house— "stay and work for us. We are weavers of cloth and need some help around the house."

Misfortune accepted gladly, and the other young women in the house welcomed her in their midst. Everything was all right for a while. Misfortune was a good housekeeper and every nook and cranny in the house was spick-n-span.

One evening, the weavers told her: "Misfortune, we are going out. We are locking the door from the outside. Your task is to keep watch and make sure nobody steals our precious work."

Misfortune nodded and off the weavers went.

During the night, Misfortune heard the noise of scissors cutting cloth. She hurried to the spot where the loom, the weft and cloth were, and saw an old woman with unkempt hair cutting all the cloth and unravelling all the weft. Can you imagine Misfortune's horror? She begged the old woman to stop, but the latter said:

"I am your ill-fortune and I will never stop."

Misfortune realised that her evil Fate really was following her everywhere and her heart sank.

When the weavers came back, they saw all their work undone and scattered on the ground, and got angry at Misfortune.

"What have you done, wretch! Is this your way of thanking us for taking you among us?" And they kicked her out of their house.

Misfortune cried for a while, but then she dried her tears, knowing that crying would not help her out of her plight, and resumed her wanderings.

One day, Misfortune arrived at a new village. She sat down next to a wine shop and asked for alms. The shopkeeper's wife gave her bread and cheese and a glass of wine. Then, her husband took pity on the girl and told his wife to let her sleep on the sacks on the shop's floor, for they slept upstairs. Misfortune was very grateful for their hospitality.

In the middle of the night, Misfortune woke up because of the smashing of glass and saw her evil Fate at her hideous work. The old hag uncorked all the caskets and let the wine run on the floor, while also smashing the glass bottles.

"Please, stop!"—Misfortune shouted, but the hag was ruthless and full of rage. When the shopkeepers came downstairs because of the commotion and saw what had happened, they blamed Misfortune, for there was no trace of her evil Fate.

"Is this your way of showing your gratitude?"—said the shopkeeper. "You have ruined us!" And in saying so, he took a stick, and beat Misfortune with all his might, and finally kicked her out of his shop. Now Misfortune really was in the pit of despair and thought her life was utterly worthless. She cried and cried, for she did not know how she could ever be free of her evil Fate.

After crying for a good while, Misfortune decided she would live alone in the woods, so that she could not harm anyone. As she wandered through the woods, she came to a ford where she saw a beautiful, sturdy woman washing and rinsing linen and clothes. The woman had strength in her arms and sang while working.

When Misfortune approached her, she looked up.

"Hello"—said the woman—"what is your name and why do you look so dejected?"

Misfortune said: "Misfortune is my name and I have endured a bitter, cruel fate."

The woman thought for a moment, then she said: "Can you iron and starch? I could use some help."

"I certainly can, but I must warn you..."

Misfortune told her story to the woman, whose name was Donna Francisca and she did the prince's laundry. Donna Francisca listened carefully, then put her hands on her hips and said:

"Don't you worry; I am not afraid!"

And she led Misfortune to her house.

Misfortune could starch and iron beautifully, and when she was done, Donna Francisca brought back the laundry to court. The prince was astounded.

"You have never done the laundry so beautifully, Donna Francisca. Here are ten golden coins to reward you for your work."

Donna Francisca used the money to buy flour and some clothes for Misfortune. Then she baked two ring-shaped loaves and instructed the girl in this way:

"Go down to the beach and call for my Fate, ask for the Fate of Donna Francisca three times. When she emerges from the waves, launch one of the loaves and greet her gently on my behalf; then ask her politely where you can find your Fate."

Misfortune hesitated. She was quite scared after all she had endured. However, Donna Francisca pushed her forward, and off the girl went.

When she arrived at the beach, Misfortune stopped on the shore and called out as she had been instructed. From the waves emerged a beautiful, sturdy woman with fiery hair, looking every bit as Donna Francisca, only larger.

"Hail to you, I give you Donna Francisca's regards," Misfortune said, throwing one of the loaves in the waves. Donna Francisca's Fate beamed with pleasure and asked Misfortune how she could help her.

The girl said: "Could you please tell me where I can find my fate?"

Donna Francisca's Fate answered: "Go back to the crossroads and take the left path. At the end of it, you will see a shabby hut. There, lives your Fate. She will snarl at you, for she is an old poor hag, but don't give up. Give her your other loaf and talk to her kindly. Then, be gone."

Misfortune thanked Donna Francisca's Fate. She found the hut easily enough. When she approached it, she kindly offered the loaf to the old hag, who had unkempt, knotty hair, was blear-eyed, had only a few teeth left and was smelly.

"Who asked you for anything?" She snapped at the girl.

Misfortune left the loaf on the window sill and said bye politely. She went back to Donna Francisca's house.

The second time Donna Francisca brought back the laundry to the prince, she was rewarded with ten more golden coins. Again, she bought some finery for Misfortune and baked a loaf with anise seeds. Misfortune brought the loaf to her Fate, and this time the old hag did not reject her.

The third time, Donna Francisca was rewarded with twenty pieces of gold. This time she bought flour, finery, pomades, and a comb. Then, she gave Misfortune the usual loaf, the comb, and some pomade to disentangle the hair of Misfortune's Fate.

Misfortune set off early in the morning. When she arrived at the hut, she saw with delight that the hag had eaten the previous loaves. At that point, she took heart and when she greeted her Fate, she gave her the third loaf and offered to comb her hair. The hag let her do so, and accepted her gifts silently. When Misfortune had combed and put pomade on her hair, the Fate said:

"You have been so kind to me that I will give you a gift."

She took a tiny box and put it in Misfortune's hands. Misfortune thanked her and ran home, eager to show the gift to Donna Francisca. When they opened it, they saw a small piece of braid, and were both disappointed. "What a small piece of nothing!" they said, and forgot it in the back of a drawer.

After some time, it happened that the prince was about to marry. When Donna Francisca went to visit him, he was quite upset. He told Donna Francisca that his bride-to-be and everyone at court was in turmoil, as the bride's dress missed a piece of braid and the like of it was nowhere to be found.

Donna Francisca understood at once and asked the prince to wait for her as she ran home to fetch the piece of braid. When she gave it to the prince, it matched the bridal dress perfectly.

"You have saved my wedding ceremony"—said the prince. "I will give you the weight in gold of this piece of braid."

To everyone's astonishment, no amount of gold the prince put on the scales could match the weight of the tiny piece of braid.

"How is this possible?"—asked the prince. "Now, Donna Francisca, there is more to this than meets the eye. Tell me the truth."

Donna Francisca had no choice but tell the whole story, and when the prince asked to meet Misfortune, Donna Francisca had her dressed in finery.

Misfortune was, after all, a king's daughter, and she remembered how to behave at court. Thus, she met the prince and told him what she had endured.

The first thing the prince did was to repay the damage the weavers and the shopkeepers had done. He also rebuked them for the harsh way they had treated Misfortune and dismissed them without further ado. Then he dismissed his betrothed too and married Misfortune instead. Donna Francisca became her dame of honour. Finally, on hearing that the king of Spain had regained his throne and family, he sent news to the castle and endeavoured to have the Spanish royal family meet Misfortune.

There was great rejoicing in both reigns. The queen and the sisters, and the king of Spain all embraced Misfortune and cried abundant tears. And they all lived in peace and abundance for many years to come.

Themes and Motifs

When I first heard the tale, I liked it very much. I jumped with recognition the moment when Misfortune meets Donna Francisca's larger-than-life Fate emerging from the waves. No doubt I rooted for Donna Francisca and her Fate also because they share my name. I was reminded of myself as a child standing at the seashore, while the waves crashed and roared. I could certainly identify with that precious moment.

However, there was more than that. The tale told by a skilled storyteller thoroughly communicated to me a sense of destiny and a sense of purpose bigger than myself; I felt called by name and singled out for a specific and unique vocation, that of storyteller and writer that facilitates emotional healing through storywork. I could feel the urgency and the enthusiasm of such a call that clearly bore my name. Here was something I had to do with my unique set of skills, talents, knowledge, and experiences. It was as if the story had worked its transmission in me, and I was receptive enough to let it come through my being. This book is part of such an endeavour; it belongs to my body of work to make this world more beautiful and whole, one reader at a time.

The way of stories in my life has never been linear. On the contrary, it has always been meandering and spiral-like, leading me to the same—yet renewed—places again and again, making me aware of how everything, including myself, changes in fundamental ways, while remaining their own selves.

The tale of Misfortune illustrates the duality of fate and destiny beautifully. The queen can represent the resourceful feminine inside ourselves. When at the market, she selects figs, the theme of communal belonging and co-creation is foregrounded, since she shows compassion for the beggar, even if she cannot give her money. The queen's unlucky daughter will have a life of poverty, isolation, and contempt for a long while, an ordeal that she is willing to go through alone. Yet, she fails miserably till Donna Francisca, her mentor and guide, comes along, thus pointing to the need for meaningful interaction and companionship both with one's Fate and with other people.

In the beginning, when the queen and her daughters have to fend for themselves, we do not know their names. We only know that they come from a royal family. Only when the queen and the youngest daughter learn about the case of their bad luck, does the latter take on the name "Misfortune". She accepts her fate and sets off. However, this is not enough. Twice her evil Fate derails her attempts at decent living in the community. It is only when Donna Francisca comes along and becomes her mentor that Misfortune accepts to look for her Fate and to face her with kindness and compassion. Thus, the tale is about how a bad fate can turn into a good destiny, as much as the facing of one's own Shadow, which works havoc when it is not acknowledged and integrated meaningfully into one's life. The Shadow is our blind spot; it is always following us, as a proper shadow would, and it includes all the aspects of ourselves we are not ready to acknowledge and own. Instead, we attribute these traits to others: people, environments, communities. The Shadow is as much individual as it is collective. When entire communities project their unaccepted fears and foibles onto individuals or other groups, isolation and persecution follow, and scapegoating is close by. We sadly have had many examples throughout history, both past and present.

Donna Francisca, on the other hand, represents the wise guide or the practical guiding wisdom that knows intuitively what needs to be done. As she is in touch with her own Fate, who looks like her (meaning there has been an integration and an ongoing dialogue between them), she knows how to obtain precious knowledge to help Misfortune out of her plight.

Donna Francisca is first met at a ford, doing the laundry for the prince. She is both a wise woman and an independent woman. Little by little, Misfortune gets acquainted with her own Fate and she receives a tiny, seemingly insignificant reward from her: a piece of braid, which turns out to be the solution to all her trials and pains. The evil Fate gives Misfortune this little gift that propels her toward her true destiny as a princess. It is again Donna Francisca that saves the situation when she quickly realises that the tiny piece of braid is the needed, missing piece. She represents a strong, healthy intuition, or intuitive wisdom.

Sometimes, in our lives, we put on a brave face and go our own ways; however, we do not really engage in shadow work, which allows us to withdraw our projections and stop the drama, shame, and blame games in our lives. We are too busy living from day to day, we have to make a living and make sure we fit in within society. Yet, all our inner baggage gets drawn along each step of the way and we are only half-aware of it, till we really face and dive deep into our pain.

The wound caused by the perception of not being enough or worthless needs to be acknowledged with compassion. In the story, it takes Misfortune two terrible misadventures before she meets Donna Francisca, and things start to turn around. It is only when she gets in touch with something bigger than her day-to-day self, when she asks for help from the numinous, that she can confront her evil Fate.

The moment Misfortune converses with the prince and tells him all she went through is the moment we take stock of our own experiences, of where we have been, before our royal self. It is the moment we are finally united to our true destiny when we no longer take in a bad fate passively; we are now ready to take our lives into our hands, take responsibility, and meet and welcome our true destiny.

Indeed, the polarity of fate and destiny is very important, as it plays a key role in any individual life. We each come into the world in different circumstances and with differing degrees of awareness. Sometimes, we get robbed or deprived of our vocations, our sense of destiny. Fate sets in. It involves our lack of awareness, our being only half-awake. We go forward blundering here and there, without a true sense of purpose and direction, till we cannot take it anymore.

In the darkest moment, when we are most lonely, we might be "lucky" enough to hear the whispers of our intuition, either by ourselves or through some other agent or object. Our souls may be thirsty for the truth of who we are. Thus, we listen. If we take on the deep work required, which entails sorting out the knotted mass of recriminations, projections, self-deprecations and the like, we may eventually come into our own domains and reach the stage where our destiny calls our name and we are able to step up to it boldly.

All of this can take time. Yet, there is hope, as the work of the soul is never finished. Once we come into our own sovereignty, we can experience integration within ourselves and within a community. This is what happens to Misfortune at the end of the tale, when she regains her family and status and also becomes the prince's bride.

In the story, we never learn the true name of Misfortune. I like to think that each of us can reach a point when we hear and claim our true name inwardly. When we over-identify with our pain, we get so entangled in it that we lose our perspective on what is going on and what needs to be done. We need to confront fate with compassion, yet, we also have to keep a cool-headed detachment to think clearly and observe thoroughly. In fact, only through keen observation can insight and breakthrough follow. To access intuition and be able to turn fate into destiny, we cannot be totally sucked into the drama vortex; awareness is key. We need to make space to allow for silence and time to work things through and take the right action through soul-aligned choices.

Creative Process Activities

Activity n. 1

For this activity, you need the following: meditative music, two large, flat, smooth stones, a sheet of paper, two pens of different colours. First of all, find a place in nature, or indoors, where you will not be disturbed. Make sure you take care of any responsibilities you might have in advance.

If possible, sit on the floor or on the ground, otherwise, a comfortable chair will do. Breathe deeply at least three times, focusing on your breath and on your physical sensations while doing so. When you are ready, play your music for at least ten minutes, better if it is ambient or any relaxing music without lyrics.

As you relax, contemplate the events or circumstances of your life up to this moment, as if in a movie. When you are ready, write down examples of your Fate on your sheets, moments when you have felt victimised in your life. Write down everything in as much detail as you can. When you are finished, select one of the stones, which is going to represent your Fate, and put your notes under the stone.

Once again, breathe deeply. Then, take a clean sheet of paper and the other pen and reminisce about moments in your life when you have felt in charge, with a clear sense of purpose and a clear mission to accomplish. If nothing comes up—which is unlikely—ask yourself the following questions more than once, till you feel compelled to write all the answers down:

> "What is my Destiny?" "How do I recognize it?"

When you are finished with your answers, fold the sheet and put it under the other stone, which represents your Destiny.

After some time spent in quiet contemplation, let your mind drift. Finally, if you are outdoors, you can choose to bury or throw your Fate stone and the connected notes into a body of water, such as a river. If you are inside, you can tear the notes and dispose of them, while you can throw the Fate stone in nature later. Then, take care of your destiny stone; burn the notes and scatter the ashes in nature. Keep your Destiny stone on your desk or in a place where you can see it often and be reminded of your true Destiny. Own it and claim it for yourself. The Present is the gate to the Future.

Activity n. 2

At another time, go to a natural place you love, bring your meditative music, and stand with your arms along your body, and your legs open at shoulder-width. Take in the sounds, smells, sights, and wind... stand like this, till you feel your feet being rooted into the earth and your head is up above, into the air element. When you feel you are listening with your whole body and being, close your eyes and ask yourself aloud or mentally: "What is my true name?"

Wait for the answer. Listen to your true name. It may come at once or at length. When you receive it, make a note and treasure it. Keep it secret.

Activity n. 3

For the following activity, you will need paper, pens, brushes, indelible paints or markers, your Destiny stone, and your true inner name.

Write down your true name on paper, then play at transforming it into a symbol that contains its essence for you. You can do this through sigil magic or simply draw a symbol that encodes the essence of your true inner name in your mind.

When you are satisfied with your symbol, paint it on the surface of your Destiny stone, using the colours you prefer. Allow the painting process to be mind-shifting, by approaching it with awareness. Let your hand draw and paint very slowly and take in each single movement, trait, and detail.

Chapter Three

The Ugly Duckling

It was a beautiful, bright summer. The corn glistened in the sunlight and the farm yard was full of life. There were ducks, poultry, cats, dogs, and rabbits everywhere.

Mother duck had been hatching her eggs for weeks, and at last, they all broke except one. Her children, the little ducklings, were lovely and graceful and all swam in a row in the pond, following her.

When the last egg finally broke, out came an ugly, grey duckling, big and awkward. His brothers and sisters exclaimed at once: “He is not like us! He is so ugly and big, mama!”

The mother duck was sorry for him, but she also felt it would have been better for him never to be born.

One day, she led her ducklings to the old, highest born duck, after instructing the little ones about polite etiquette. The old duck uttered her verdict: “They are all pretty enough, except for that one, my dear! It is so big and ugly!”

The ugly duckling was mortified and would have disappeared, if only had it been possible. All the poultry made fun of him and pecked him in the neck; the girl who fed the hens kicked him out of her way.

He felt so lonely and miserable that he left the farm. He flew till he reached a moor where some wild geese lived. They let him stay there, but wanted nothing to do with him.

One day, there was a booming sound all around and flocks of geese fell dead to the ground. Hunters were everywhere and their hounds were set loose.

The ugly duckling was terrified and covered his eyes with his wings. A hound saw him and passed him by.

"I am so grateful", he thought, "for I am so ugly that not even hounds would chase me."

Summer slowly turned to autumn, with its golden and orange hues. The ugly duckling saw some white, beautiful, big birds for the first time. They were swans. They were so elegant and beautiful as they stretched their necks and flew to the South for the winter! They produced a strange, uncanny sound, as they flew by. The ugly duckling was mesmerised.

He felt a strange pang in his heart. It was not envy, though, but joy for the existence of such graceful creatures.

"How I wish I could follow you!" he thought.

Soon winter arrived and snow and ice followed in its tracks. The ugly duckling kept on swimming in a circle to keep the surface of the pond from freezing. At last, the water was completely frozen and his legs were stuck in the ice. He was half-dead. Besides, he had almost starved to death. He wished he would die there and then.

A farmer saw him and took pity. He freed him and brought him home, where the warmth revived him a little, but the noisy children scared him so much that he flew away.

Soon a storm swept the countryside. The ugly duckling came near a cottage whose door had an opening he could go through. When he did so, he met a tomcat and a hen who started to purr and clack, taking turns. Their owner, an old woman, thought he was able to lay eggs and let him stay there.

The tomcat and the hen were full of themselves. They thought their little world to be the whole universe. In Spring, the ugly duckling felt he needed a good, refreshing swim and when he said so, the cat and the hen disparaged him for his stupidity. He felt so lonely and misunderstood again!

He flew out and swam across the river.

When he looked up with eyes full of tears, he saw the beautiful swans coming back across the sky, after the winter. His heart leapt with longing and joy. How beautiful they were!

"I will go to them and let them kill me, for they are so beautiful they won't have anything to do with me. Better be killed by them than picked upon, scorned and disparaged by ducks, poultry and geese, or to starve to death in winter!"

Meanwhile, the swans were gliding on the surface of the river.

He swam in their direction, and they all came towards him.

He was expecting to be attacked to death. Instead, they all flew around him, to welcome him and stroked his neck. As he bent, he saw his own reflection in the water: he too was a swan!

Now children threw bread and cake in the water and cried in delight: "Look! There is a new one! He is the youngest and the most beautiful of them all!"

And, indeed, all other swans paid their homage to him.

The ugly duckling, now a swan, was deeply moved and happy, but not in the least proud, and exclaimed: "I never even dreamed of such happiness when I was an ugly duckling!"

Themes and Motifs

When I was a child, there was a fortnightly fairy and folk tale magazine for children, complete with audio cassettes. I first listened to and read 'The Ugly Duckling' through that remarkable combination of wonderful illustrations and expressive readings. The readers were professional theatre actors.

I re-read the tale years later in Hans Christian Andersen's collection and have had an affinity for this melancholic tale at every single re-reading.

My third encounter with *'The Ugly Duckling'* happened in my twenties, when I picked up *Women Who Run with the Wolves* by Dr. Clarissa Pinkola Estés. This time, when I read the tale out loud to myself, my voice faltered, and my sight blurred because of tears. I could not help myself. *'The Ugly Duckling'* hit where it hurt, in the very core of my isolation and estrangement.

I had been undergoing a peeling off and exposure of my sense of self. Through a set of complicated circumstances, I ended up feeling in exile in the midst of daily life.

The ugly duckling that finally found his pack moved me and warmed my heart with hope for the future. Something inside me literally shifted and I experienced the healing power of the story.

'The Ugly Duckling' is about the wound of not belonging, of being different, therefore rejected, avoided, or scorned. It is about the wound of being considered weird, strange, unfit for the mundane contexts we live in.

The pain and ordeals the little duckling goes through are the price we pay when confronted with set, unconscious ways, which have long been established and taken for granted in stagnant and self-complacent social contexts. It is the price paid by those who do not fit the criteria, those who are "too little" or "too much".

The tale also is about growth and deepened sensibility through the pains of experience. The ugly duckling becomes a beautiful swan, while keeping his humility and gratitude: he is able to enjoy his happiness all the more because of his previous painful experiences. We also are told that at times the ugly duckling is grateful for being so, because hounds won't pursue him and are inclined to leave him alone.

The tale deals with exile as a condition for the growth of the soul, and with the pang of recognition and joy of finding one's true and elective family. *'The Ugly Duckling'* is a tale for the outsiders inside us. It depicts the way the world conditions us into thinking badly of ourselves. We end up believing the lies about being unworthy and ugly in more than one sense; we are fed by an unsympathetic environment.

The motif of the bird as a symbol of the soul is found in fairy and folk tales all over the world. The same can be said about the motif of the misfit, the ostracised and exiled. This "damnatio memoriae" some of us have to deal with is a terrible condition of alienation from the world we are trying to belong to, except that we do not. As a consequence, we are forced inward, into an inner descent.

When, at some point, spring comes, we have transformed and we, as well as others, realise it at once. To grow our souls, some of us have to undergo this kind of ordeal at quite a young age. We feel, and indeed are, different from our peers. We do not conform and they resent us. Thus, we prefer to withdraw in ourselves.

When time is ripe, we are called to step forth fully transformed: we can be graceful and compassionate, elegant and humble, beautiful and grateful at the same time, overcome by deep joy. This is the experience of the ugly duckling, of the young one that undergoes many trials and is later called to be a leader of sorts just by being his or her beautiful self.

All other swans pay homage to the most beautiful and welcome him among them: the tale is also about the need for a true, authentic community and the sweet joy of recognition. Finding our pack can make all the difference between life and death, barely surviving and blossoming and blooming into the fullness of who we are.

When I read or tell *'The Ugly Duckling'*, I am reminded of two famous poems: *The Rime of the Ancient Mariner*, first written in 1798 by Samuel T. Coleridge, and 'The Albatross', included in the second edition (1861) of Charles Baudelaire's poetic collection *Les Fleurs du Mal.*

They both feature an albatross. In the former, the ancient mariner slays the albatross, thus bringing misfortune upon himself and his companions. In Coleridge's poem, the albatross is an embodiment of the benevolence of nature. When the mariner kills it, all sorts of evils befall the crew. In Baudelaire's interpretation, the albatross is a scapegoat and represents the Poet.

The bird is the king of the blue sea and sky. It is as beautiful in its flight as it is awkward on earth, where its big wings prevent it from walking. This motif also appears in *'The Ugly Duckling'*, awkward because of his large wings.

The love for our ideas and values is what makes us reach the sublime heights of feeling and imagination, but also what makes us targets of disparagement, hatred, ridicule, or perplexity. This is the quintessential condition of the Poet as an archetype; it is the way some introverted, sensitive, empathetic individuals approach life and the world.

While the Poet feels heightened joy and ecstasy, she also experiences deeper suffering than most. In a materialistic society, the Poet is ridiculed because her values and sensitivity undermine its set ways and laws. The Poet as an archetype embodies subtle, emotional perceptiveness and authenticity.

"The Ugly Duckling', which is, in truth, a swan, also deals with the need of finding oneself through self-discovery and true community. He prefers approaching the swans, for whom he feels love and affinity, risking rejection and even death, to a petty existence of endless vexations. There is a sort of heroic attitude at play. His authentic nature calls him out and he dares to approach the swans.

The tale also is about going beyond limited beliefs, perceptions, values, and opinions. All the other animals in the story have fixed ideas about the world and their roles in it. They project their preconceptions, based on their circumscribed experiences, on the protagonist, therefore expecting him to conform to their own views and prejudices. He, however, cannot do so and, before joining the swans, flies away on his own each single time.

Creative Process Activities

The following activities inspired by the theme of *'The Ugly Duckling'* aim at developing a strong sense of self-awareness.

Activity n. 1: Hidden Poem

Set 10 minutes aside when you can be alone and undisturbed. Sit with an upright back, comfortable and relaxed. Begin by focusing on your breath, or on the flame of a candle. Have your journal and pen handy.

For the following activity, re-read the tale and, every ten lines, pick the fifth word of each line. Then, among all the words you selected in this way, choose one: this will be the title of a poem you will write with the remaining words you selected.

Play with the words. For example, if you have selected "bright" and "thought", you can also modify them: "bright" can become "brightness" and "thought" can become "thoughtless" or "thoughtful". In other words, if you have an adjective, you can transform it into a noun and vice-versa; if you have a noun, it can become a verb, or a verb can become a noun. As long as you keep the root of the word, you can change its function in the sentence.

Arrange the words you chose in a way that feels poetic or original to you. Then, see if you can find or make up a hidden meaning in the arranged words. Add connectors, such as "and", "but", "even if" and all the words you need to express your insights.

Work on your poem playfully; add and subtract as much as you need to. When you are satisfied with the result, or have a feeling of closure, rewrite your poem with a coloured pen and a beautiful handwriting. Sign and preserve it in your journal.

After one day, re-read your poem and journal about what it means to you.

How is it related to your current life situation or to the way you feel?

Use the poem as a springboard for your reflections.

Activity n. 2: Journaling Prompts

When have you felt an ugly duckling? Describe the situation(s).

How did you respond? How did you come out of that?

Have you found the silver lining in your situation?

What would you tell your ugly duckling self, if you were your best friend?

Take as little or as long as you need with this process. Don't rush.

Activity n. 3: Letter to Self

Meditate for 10 minutes with your eyes closed. Then, write a letter to yourself.

Start with:

Dear Self,

Thank you for ______________________________

List all the reasons why you are indeed grateful to yourself. It is important to be specific and to acknowledge ourselves through gratitude. You can list both past and present circumstances you are grateful for.

Next, offer support, imagining that you are older and wiser than now. Give some possible, positive tips to yourself. How could you act to acknowledge a specific situation? And what actions could you take to tackle an issue?

Finally, date and sign your letter and keep it safe.

Extra Tip:

If you enjoyed writing a letter to yourself, repeat the practice once a week, as a beautiful way to check in with yourself and gauge the undercurrents of feelings flowing through your life.

It can become an ongoing practice of self-empowerment and gratitude, training yourself to shift perspectives.

Section II
Tests and Trials

Chapter Four

Beauty and the Beast

'Beauty and the Beast' is a very popular tale first written by Madame Gabrielle-Suzanne Barbot de Villeneuve, a French woman writer who lived in Paris between 1685 and 1755. Despite having become famous thanks to Disney, it still holds hidden pearls of wisdom. Various writers have re-imagined it, changing many of its details. Angela Carter's version is only one notable case. On my part, instead, I have chosen not to modify the plot.

There was once a rich merchant who had seven daughters and sons. They led a splendid life in town till the day their father lost all his merchant ships at sea through shipwreck, fire, and pirates.

When he learned about what had happened, the merchant had no choice but to have his children move to a desolate house in the midst of a dark forest, where they had to work hard to make ends meet because they no longer had servants or friends.

The daughters were really distressed, except one, the youngest, who put on a cheerful face and tried to find the good in everything. She was the most beautiful and clever of all, and her father and brothers, who loved her dearly, called her Beauty.

After about two years since their downfall, the merchant came to know that one of his lost ships had been retrieved, so he intended to go to town and make inquiries about it.

All rejoiced and thought they were going to be rich again, so they wanted to buy new clothes, jewels, and other leisure objects. The merchant, however, was more cautious, and so was Beauty.

When their father asked what he should bring them, the daughters asked for grand things, such as jewels and finery, whereas Beauty kept silent. Her father insisted on fulfilling one of her wishes, so she only asked for a pink rose.

The merchant set out and when he arrived in town, he found out that his associates, believing him dead, had divided the cargo and the profits among themselves. Thus, he continued to be poor and could not afford to buy the expensive presents his daughters had requested.

He set out to go back as soon as possible, but the weather was so stormy that he had to stop on his journey and find a shelter to spend the night. The best he could find was a hollow in a big tree and there he tried to sleep, but the howling of the wolves kept him awake.

In the morning, he got out of the hollow trunk and saw with relief that the mist had cleared and the surrounding countryside was colourful and pleasant.

In the evening, while on his way, he saw a splendid castle on a hilltop and since the sun was setting below the horizon, he hastened in its direction. He felt reassured and thought that the lord of such a splendid castle would give him hospitality.

As he walked along a broad path edged with elder trees, he noticed the beauty and sweet fragrances of the countryside. When he arrived at the castle gate, he was surprised to see it open and let him pass through. At first, he hesitated, since he could not see anyone, but then he took heart and went forward.

The same happened when he went into the castle's main hall. As he walked, admiring all the splendid richness of the interior, he passed through many rooms and halls, each one different yet sumptuously decorated, each more beautiful than the last. The merchant was troubled because he could not see anybody around.

He arrived in a large room with a big fireplace and sofa and, next to it, a laid table with all the dainty food and drink he could wish for. He looked around to see whether his kind host would reveal his presence, but he was alone.

He waited and waited, till hunger and tiredness overcame him, due to his long journey; thus, he ate at the table and fell asleep on the sofa.

When he woke up, the sun was already high in the sky. His breakfast was on the table, so he sat up and ate it with a good appetite. He would have liked to thank his host, but there was no one. Therefore, he decided to resume his journey so that he could reach his home and children within the day.

As he crossed the heavenly gardens surrounding the castle, he saw there were rose bushes at each side of the path and was reminded of Beauty's request. He would at least fulfil her desire, for surely no one would mind if he picked up one of those beautiful pink roses, and so he did.

He had scarcely chosen and cut his rose with his knife, that the blood curled in his veins, as he heard a beastly snarl.

A ferocious, gruff voice said: "Who told you to steal my roses? Was I not kind enough to you?"

An awful, furry beast towered in front of the merchant, who tried to contain his terror as best as he could.

"You will die!" said the beast.

At that, the merchant started the story of his misfortunes and asked for forgiveness, but the beast, who had been listening, said:

"On one condition only can you save your head! Bring me one of your daughters! But beware: she must come willingly within one month, otherwise I will come and fetch you in your own house."

The poor merchant trembled to his very core and was full of sorrow at the very thought of giving away one of his daughters. Besides, he doubted that any of them would go to the beast willingly.

He set out on a black stead with a chest full of jewels and finery that the beast had prepared for the merchant's journey, and he also held the pink rose for Beauty.

Alas, had she only known what a single rose had cost, she would never have asked for it!

In the evening, the merchant reached his house in the forest and his sons and daughters all rejoiced in seeing him again, in good health and carrying finery and riches. They assumed his business in town had turned out for the best, and they were all very rich again, but when Beauty came forward to welcome him back, the poor father broke into tears and gave her the rose, saying it was the costliest rose in the world. Then, he told his children all that had happened to him.

On hearing of the beast, they were sorrowful and the sons made plans to kill the beast, should he come near their father, who was by then convinced that there was no escape from their plight. They were all miserable then.

The eldest sisters were all angry at Beauty for, had she had a more sensible request, such misfortune would not have happened in the first place. Beauty rose and told her brothers and sisters:

"I certainly am guilty for our misfortune, but never could I have imagined to bring it about by asking for a simple rose! Therefore, I am ready to go to the beast."

At that, her father and brothers protested vehemently, for they really loved her; but her heart was set.

When the time came, Beauty and the merchant set out on their journey to the beast's castle. At first, the beast did not show itself, so that they could make themselves comfortable. The morning after, however, as soon as they had had their breakfast, he appeared to welcome Beauty and send her father back.

Beauty was struck with terror, first at his voice and then at his ferocious appearance; however, when he asked her whether she had come willingly, she greeted him politely and said that indeed she had.

The beast was pleased and gave orders that the merchant should leave after choosing as many precious gifts for his sons and daughters as he could fit in a big wooden chest. Beauty was to help him fill it.

And so it was, that after seeing to that, Beauty and her father had to part. Beauty shed a tear, for she knew she would never see her father again, while the latter, on his part, persuaded himself that maybe he would be able to visit her from time to time, and set off at the beast's bidding.

In the following hours and days, Beauty was to discover the many charms and entertainments of the castle, where she came across many rooms with magical mirrors, speaking parrots and other birds, musical instruments, huge libraries and wonderful gardens, full of rare flowers and her favourite roses.

Every day, despite her solitude, she would find ways to entertain herself through the wonders of the castle. In the evening, after she had eaten her supper, the beast would come and inquire about her day and how she felt.

Beauty told him what she had done wholeheartedly, for she preferred the beast's company to being alone all the time. At the end of the conversation, the beast would ask her:

"Beauty, will you marry me?"

The first time he asked, she was taken aback and was afraid to answer for fear of his reaction, but since he insisted on receiving a sincere answer, she answered, "No, I won't." Thus, seeing that the beast did not get angry, Beauty answered in the same way every evening, and stopped being afraid, for the beast was not so terrible after all.

At night, Beauty would dream of a beautiful location in the castle that she still had to discover. There, a handsome prince was allegedly a prisoner of the beast. In the dream, the prince always looked sad and reproachful and told her not to mind appearances. Then, a beautiful lady would also appear, telling Beauty not to be deceived by appearances.

This dream happened every night and, in the morning, Beauty was sad to wake up, as she missed her handsome prince.

She was puzzled by the lady's advice. Invariably, she would discover the physical location of the dream from the previous night, which changed every time, but there never was any trace of the handsome prince.

...Time went by, and Beauty grew melancholic, for she missed her father and family and wished to see them once again.

When the Beast asked her what the matter was, she was brave enough and told him:

"I wish I could see my father one last time. If only you sent me to him for two months, I promise I will come back and stay here for the rest of my life."

The Beast sighed and said:

"I love you so much that I can't deny you anything. I will let you go, but beware, keep your promise, for by the end of two months, if you don't come back, your Beast will be dead."

He gave her a magic ring that, once spoken to, would bring her back in the blink of an eye. Beauty promised she would keep her word. Then, she was happy to prepare new gifts for her family.

That night she dreamed of her Prince being very sad, lying on the ground dying.

"Ah, Beauty! How can you do this to me?" he said.

When she woke up in the morning, she was upset; yet, she convinced herself that it had only been an idle dream and set off on her journey.

When she arrived home in the evening, her father and brothers rejoiced greatly and they asked her many questions.

She gave precious gifts to her sisters and was happy to have two months to spend with them all.

Time flew by, and ten days before the time was up, she started to miss her Beast, and his polite and caring conversation. Two nights before the end of the two months, she dreamed of the prince dying and heard the lady tell her that the time was almost up and she should hurry, if she cared for the Beast. He would soon be dead.

Beauty was confused and spoke to her ring.

At the castle, she ran inside and called out to the Beast.

Since he did not appear, she grew very worried and ran down the stairs, into the rose garden, where she had seen the dying Prince in her dream.

She ran and ran in the labyrinth, holding up her long gown. Finally, she reached the very heart of the maze, where to her horror, she saw the Beast lying on the ground.

Beauty dropped to her knees, breaking into sobs and tears:

"Dear Beast, how I have missed you and how I love you! Please, do not die! Is it too late?"

She pleaded in despair. As she uttered those words, burying her face in the Beast's fur, all the roses in the garden turned a vibrant, deep red. She cried and cried, till something started to change.

The Beast's fur disappeared and his face and body turned into those of the handsome Prince who had visited her dreams. He opened his eyes.

I cannot tell you the crazy joy Beauty felt, but in truth, had he stayed a Beast, she would have felt the same.

They embraced. The prince was still weak. The beautiful lady from the dream appeared too:

"You have come just on time. Had you waited longer, you would have found the prince dead. Now, it is time to rejoice, for you have broken the curse and restored the prince to his human form. The Queen, his mother, will be deeply happy and grateful for your true heart."

And so it was that after a few days, the lady of the dream, who was none other than a fairy godmother, had Beauty's father, brothers and sisters come to the royal wedding of Beauty and the Prince, who lived happily and in love for many years to come.

Themes and Motifs

At the beginning of the tale, the merchant and his children move into a house in the middle of a dark forest, which can be considered a place of isolation and transformation through inner and outer work. The family has lost both riches and social connections. They are all very upset, except for Beauty, who tries to find the silver lining in their circumstances.

When there may be a possibility of recovering part of the family riches, Beauty is not enticed by the promise of new wealth. The time of dwelling in the forest has taught her caution. However, her simple request for a rose brings about further misfortune.

Beauty is the one who changes. Her process of transformation and her humility eventually equip her with what is needed to face and live with the Beast. Her self-sacrifice must be chosen; she must exert her free will, if the curse is to be broken at all. Moreover, the motif of the precious gifts the Beast provides for Beauty's family represents something of herself, a pledge of her devotion and love for them, instead of being only an exchange price for Beauty's stay at the castle.

The rose has always been an emblem of what is most beautiful, daintiest, purest in life. It crosses the border between sacred and profane, eroticism and platonic or ideal love. It is associated with the Divine Feminine and with its main symbolic embodiment in the Christian tradition, the Virgin Mary. The rose also signifies spiritual and mystical knowledge, accessing higher wisdom and visionary levels of consciousness, contacting the divine. Thus, such a seemingly simple object, a rose, is the symbol of the highest aspirations of spirituality, beauty, love, and creativity at the heart of the Western mystical, cultural, and esoteric traditions. This is why in the tale, its price is so high.

The rose is an exquisite flower that also contains the spiral pattern of ideal perfection, bliss, and love, together with spiky thorns, capable of wounding, symbolising pain, sorrow, and sacrifice as the archetypal spurs to awaken. The rose is the symbolic key to the road of tests and trials, as it signifies coming to awakened consciousness through the experience of pain and the dark night of the soul.

Another important theme in the tale is that of the cursed prince turned into a beast. The latter can represent both the Shadow and the personification of fears emerging from the unconscious.

Beauty and the Beast are the two polar opposites of consciousness working towards individuation. Something has to die, and something has to transform and be joined for a new kind of awareness to be born.

The motif of deceiving appearances as misleading is more than patriarchal moralism: on the path towards the deepening of the soul, we all need to be able to discriminate and find truth, when it is not in plain sight. Indeed, this motif flows through the story like an undercurrent. It is only when Beauty is away from the castle that she realises she misses the Beast.

There have been famous re-writings of this tale, including versions where it is Beauty that turns into a furry beast to join the Beast in his dimension, and others where the Beast is such inside-out, where appearances are not deceiving and what you see is what you get.

In presenting the tale in my own words, I have kept some of the motifs of the popularised children's tale passed down through Madame de Villeneuve's and Madame de Beaumont's versions of 1740 and 1756, respectively. The latter was meant to teach girls a moral lesson, but as already noted, the motif of misleading appearances can be seen as a test on the initiatory path of the soul.

Beauty's sisters and brothers can represent more socialised selves or personas and their needs within the individual's psyche. Although ineffective, brothers are more positive than sisters, who are jealous of Beauty. On a surface level, this is the depiction of antagonism among women, the sister wound that needs to be healed in our cultures and psyches. Once acknowledged as the existence of internalised contrasting drives or needs within the psyche, the healing becomes possible.

The father and the brothers love Beauty, yet they are also ineffective and childish in their way of loving. It is the sort of love that cannot help us avoid sorrow and understand ourselves deeply. Thus, Beauty's path of trials and tests and her life at the castle are instrumental to her individual awakening.

I added the detail of the colour of the roses changing from pink to red, the moment Beauty realises her love for the Beast. At that very moment, she pierces through the veil of illusion and makes it back just on time to avoid the Beast's death. Her tears, pain, awareness, and love save him from certain death, and in the process, Beauty saves herself too. The Beast dissolves, the prince emerges.

In *'Beauty and the Beast'*, the motif of the curse, with the consequent loss of change and loss of identity is very important. The change into a beast can represent all those unredeemed inner traits and baggage we carry along in our lives up to a point, when they start to kill us slowly—or quickly. It is an involution, a shutting down something inside which we all can experience at different stages in our lives.

Whether through grief, illness, or addiction, we just cannot get a handle on our instinctual drives. It is an experience of descent, of being stuck in a dark cave, where our thwarted aspirations to light and beauty (the rose) make our pain even more poignant because of their incommensurable distance from our current conditions.

Eventually, the curse can be turned into a blessing and even be dissolved through love. Beauty's progression from being attracted to the handsome prince in her dreams to realising her love for the Beast is her—and our—initiation into the mysteries of love, both for self and others.

When she lets go of what she deems proper and beautiful, her heart connection deepens and, in my imagination, the pale pink rose turns red because of that. In the most known version, there is no mention of the colour of the rose but it seems to me a good detail to underscore the point just made.

When all of this happens—and only then—the beast becomes human again. It may seem that once the beast-like transition is over all is "back to normal", except that it is not. In fact, as good tales all over the world teach, the experience of what has been, once healed, becomes a treasure trove of wisdom and compassion.

The final wedding of Beauty and the prince represents the sacred union of the feminine and the masculine within each well-integrated individual psyche that has overcome the tests and trials met on the road: this is the alchemical process of advancing on the path to wholeness, whose ultimate prize is individuation. As Carl Gustav Jung said, the image of the anima is a man's projection on concrete women in his life, and the image of the animus is a woman's projection on concrete men; the withdrawal of projection and the integration of masculine and feminine in the psyche lead to individuation. Becoming an individual means, in fact, being 'whole' or undivided within.

Creative Process Activities: The Dance of the Feminine and the Masculine

Preparation and Meditation

Gather a blank sheet, a pen, a pencil, and an eraser.

Before starting, take some time to eliminate outer and inner distractions by finding a calm, solitary space, and breathing in and out slowly at least three times. Close your eyes.

Feel your connection to the earth through the soles of your feet and to the sky through the top of your head. Imagine your soles growing silver filaments penetrating the earth and enveloping it, while the earth's energy animates them; imagine your hair connecting and streaming into the air element, drawing in the cosmic energies of sun, moon and stars.

Feel these earth and celestial energies converge into your *hara*, the pit of your stomach, your solar plexus, and your heart. Visualise a pillar of light extending from your root to your heart, blazing and burning evenly.

After a few moments, shake your limbs, move, rotate your core and arms. Open your eyes and reconnect to the place you are in. Drink some water to ground yourself in the present moment.

It is time to sit at your desk or in a comfortable place with your materials.

Activity n. 1

Draw two human faces as silhouettes facing each other, so that you can see a chalice shape in the blank space in-between.

Flesh out the details of the faces. Decide which one is the feminine and draw its features. Draw the masculine features of the remaining face. Take your time with drawing your details.

When you are finished, observe each of the silhouettes in turn.

What adjectives and phrases come to mind when you observe the feminine? Write them down at the bottom of the sheet. Then, observe the masculine silhouette and repeat the process.

Next, join the empty chalice space between the silhouettes with two horizontal lines, marking the base and the rim of the chalice.

Place your drawing at some distance and look at it.

Now breathe in and out three times and close your eyes again. What emerges from their union? Do you feel, sense, see anything?

After a while, open your eyes, and write in the chalice what emerged for you. It may be cryptic and it may surprise or puzzle you. Allow time to process. Let information and insight seep through your consciousness in their own time, then make notes and act on them.

Taking a walk, visiting an exhibition, or going to a new place can all be good options. Be open, be ready for insight.

Activity n. 2

Sacred movement has been acknowledged as a powerful practice throughout the ages.

For this activity, your journal, pen, and some sacred music, such as Gregorian chants, Tibetan or Buddhist chants, chimes, bells, or Sufi music. You also need an incense stick. Rose or sandalwood are good fragrances to evoke the sacredness of this ritual activity. Finally, you also need comfortable clothes.

After breathing and grounding, light your incense sticks and put on the selected music.

Stand up, and if you are comfortable in doing so, close your eyes.

Feel into the music for some time, then start moving slowly. Imagine that the feminine and the masculine energies are dancing and mingling in you through your body. Listen to your body, to the way it wants to respond to the music. Imagine that the music is a river where these energies meet and merge, flowing through your whole body. Sense it and let it flow freely.

Move your arms, neck, and legs accordingly. Let the flow of the music guide your movements.

When you feel that the movement and mingling of the energies are over, stand still for a few moments; then sit down, and write your sensations, feelings, and impressions in your journal. If you want, you can also sketch your movements by making simple figures depicting the spontaneous choreography you acted out. Keep it in your journal for future reference.

Chapter Five

Tom, Tit, Tot

The following story is originally from Suffolk, England. It appeared for the first time in print in *The Ipswich Journal* in 1878 as a contribution in the local dialect by a woman named Mrs. Anna Walter-Thomas. Since then, it has been reprinted many times, with less and less dialect. Jacobs collected it in his *English Fairy Tales*, published in 1894. The tale is similar to one collected by the Grimms, whose title is 'Rumpelstiltskin'.

'Tom, Tit, Tot'

Once upon a time, there was a peasant woman who lived in the Suffolk countryside with her beautiful daughter. One day, it happened that the woman, after baking five tiny pies, put them on the window sill to cool down. After a while, her daughter opened the window and saw the little pies. She was so hungry that she ate them all and then closed the window.

When her mother found out what her daughter had done, she started to sing, "My daughter ate five pies in a day!" Close by, the king was crossing the countryside on horseback and got curious about the song, but at a distance, he could not make out the words. Sure enough, he came near the woman's cottage and asked her what the song was about.

The woman blushed, she was ashamed to tell the king what her daughter had done, so she said: "My daughter spun five skeins of flax in a day!"

The king was very surprised: "For all I know, nobody was ever able to do such a thing! Bring me your daughter, she will be my wife. She will have all she wants to eat and wear, and good company for eleven months, but in the last month of our first year of marriage, she will have to spin five skeins of flax every day, otherwise she will be put to death."

The peasant woman had no intention to let this star opportunity pass her by, and she thought there was plenty of time to sort things out, so she didn't change her account of the facts.

It so happened that the king married the peasant girl and gave her all she wanted. The peasant woman was very satisfied with herself and thought the king would forget all about his conditions, given that he was so in love with her beautiful daughter, now his queen.

When the last day of the eleventh month came, the king told his young wife: "My dear, now you have to spin five skeins of flax every day for a month, as your mother promised you could do, otherwise I will put you to death."

The poor queen was bewildered, for she had never spun in her whole life. Yet, she kept her countenance before the king. The morning after, the king led her to the top of the tower, into a small room full of flax and a little spinning wheel. He locked the door, leaving her by herself. Now, the queen was dejected and cried her eyes out, for she did not know how to come out of her plight.

As she cried, she heard a noise and she saw a pebble land on the floor from the window. She went over and leant forward. In an instant, a little back imp with a grin and a twirling tail jumped inside.

"What are you crying for?" he said.

The queen reckoned that telling him would not make any difference or harm, so she told him the whole story. He pondered her situation a while, then he said: "I will come every morning, take your flax, spin it for you and bring it back in the evening."

"What do you want in exchange?" she asked.

"I will give you three guesses a day. If you cannot guess my name by the last evening of the month, then you shall be mine," he said. His eyes burnt like coals and his grin was awful.

The queen, despite her horror, accepted his help. Every day she would give the imp her flax and she would receive it ready at dusk. Then, he would ask: "Woman, what's my name?"

The queen racked her brains for all the local names, but she never guessed right. Then, she tried unusual names, to no avail.

The last evening of the month, the king, who was by now very satisfied with his young queen, because she had not lied to him, decided to have dinner with her in the tower, so they sat together at a little table and he told her: "You know, dear, what happened to me today, while I was hunting? I was on the hilltop, pursuing a big stag, when I heard a voice coming from a deep pit. I dismounted my stead and peeped inside: there was a tiny little black man with a tail, spinning at a tiny wheel, singing to himself, "Nimini, ninimi, not, my name is Tom, Tit, Tot!" How bizarre is that, my dear?"

The young queen was so happy to hear that, that she felt like jumping around the room, but she kept quiet and waited for the king to leave her. Then, the imp arrived. When he had given her the spun flax, he said: "Now, this is your last attempt, woman. Then you shall be mine!"

The young queen pretended to be afraid. She started with two random guesses:

"Is your name Salomon?"

"No, it isn't."

"Is it Nicodemus?"

"No, it isn't. Now, woman, think carefully, for you shall be mine soon!"

The queen burst into laughter and said with her finger pointed at the imp:

"Nimini, nimini, not, your name is Tom, Tit, Tot!"

As she uttered his true name, the imp got so angry that he gave out a shriek and jumped out of the window, disappearing into the cold December night forever.

Themes and Motifs

The mother who turns her daughter's questionable behaviour into an asset with a lie that lures the king is a good image of that aspect of the ego which seeks to acquire, expand, possess, and have power. She is protective towards her inexperienced daughter, yet she pushes her out into adventure through a test. The king is the aspect of the psyche that sets a challenge, that seeks us out, and tests our resilience and resourcefulness, as well as our ability to overcome. If in the previous story what is tested is Beauty's (and our) heart, here the story tests our guts and the courage to take risks, to jump into the unknown, not being able to see far into the future but trusting that we have enough time to find the resources and solutions we need. The story is about jumping without a safety net. It also is about being ready.

It is interesting that when all seems lost, a little imp appears to help us out in exchange for our lives, for what is most precious, our freedom to be. The little imp is the predator, or evil double in our psyches, who is out to enslave us through temptation or horror. It has great energy and potential, but like Mephistopheles in Goethe's *Faust*, it embodies that power that seeks out evil and ends up producing good. Thus, it is a sinister force within the psyche, but once we know its name (its very essence), we can channel its energy and power for our goals and purposes.

The fact that the queen has three guesses at his name every night signal that this is an important aspect. In fact, in fairy tales, three is a magical number. It is the very king, who sets the mortal challenge for the queen, that provides her with the knowledge she needs to defeat the imp. This can be read as serendipity and unexpected help coming from unusual places. The self that challenges us to grow into our own sovereignty, to become queens of our own domains, is the one who provides us with the missing piece, once we have been brave and alert and grabbed our chances. Thus, both the mother and the daughter take risks, the former out of a desire for social betterment and power, the latter out of vital necessity. In both cases, the price of failure is death.

The peasant girl, who at first is only a young beautiful daughter eating pies impulsively out of hunger, grows into a beautiful, canny queen, who by the end of the story is no longer afraid and points her finger at the little imp with authority and scorn. Once she names him, he no longer has any power and disappears into the night. In all traditional societies, knowing the true name of a being or object means possessing their essence, thus having power over them. This happens in the psyche too. When we discover the predator's gimmicks, tricks, and threats, we can vanquish them and earn our sovereignty. It is at that moment, not at the beginning of our challenge, that we are able to recognize how much ground we have covered.

In the first eleven months of the marriage between the peasant woman's daughter and the king, the latter gives her all she wants, yet, he only shows her his love at the end of the last month, by dining with her in the tower, and revealing to her what happened to him while hunting, which turns out to be of pivotal importance.

This metaphorically speaks of our need to prove ourselves and stretch beyond our comfort zones, and to mobilise all we can, all our resources one by one. In the process of becoming queens of our own selves, we also mobilise resources we are not aware of having at our disposal. Thus, this also is a tale about trusting and leaping into the unknown, having faith and being ready to jump at opportunity when we are most in need, while not letting darkness and despair engulf us. Once found out, the little imp turns out to be ridiculous and powerless.

It is ok to fake it till we make it, to believe in our own possibilities and ability to grow and be up to the challenge of becoming our true selves by showing up day after day. Building trust and self-confidence inside us takes time. Yet, we build it best, the story says, while taking action and calculated risks. In the story, time is on the heroine's side twice: when her mother lies to the king and in the bargain with the little imp. This is to say that step-by-step action can open up new pathways and solutions for us, which are not known and foreseeable at first. We grow at every turn, and what we see and find at each bend of the road can surprise us. The key is to be ready, and to cultivate openness to the possible in our lives.

Sometimes, neither planning nor trying to foresee what the future holds for our lives can help us. Growth happens through tests, and often, trials. It is the way of initiation that requires us to be willing not to know in advance all the steps we need to take in our best interest. Sometimes, it will feel as mere survival, other times it will feel as sheer luck but it is serendipity, something happening at a certain time to give us help, warning, a sign, a nudge, and point us in the right direction or to course correct, while we still can.

Creative Process Activities

Activity n. 1

For this activity, you will need three 6 x 8 inches (15 x 20 cm) cardboard squares—which you can cut out yourself—adhesive tape, markers, and pens with thick and thin tips; three sheets of white paper, glue, scissors, and your journal.

First of all, take the cardboard squares and join them together to make a triptych, thus using adhesive tape at the top and at the bottom of either long side, in such a way that it is possible to fold two wings onto the central piece. Then, leave the triptych aside, and while sitting, close your eyes. Breathe in and out deeply at least three times, and ground yourself, feeling roots growing down into the earth from the soles of your feet. Then, take the blank paper and a pen.

Without ever raising the tip of your pen from the sheet, draw the portrait of your inner king, the challenger, the one that spurs you into action. Just let your hand draw freely; do not worry about jangled lines, knots, and the like. Draw in a continuous line. When you are finished, put down the pen.

Now, close your eyes again, breathe in and out at least three times, and then draw your inner imp, the dark side of the self. Again, draw in one continuous line; let the portrait emerge by itself. When you are ready, put down the pen.

Breathe again deeply and close your eyes. Now, take a pen of a different colour and in one continuous line, draw your inner, resourceful queen. Let her emerge freely, without ever raising the tip of your pen from the paper. When you have finished, draw the three portraits in greater detail, and in the blank spaces around each of them, jot down the phrases and words that come to your mind, when looking at each one in turn. Finally, glue the portrait of the king on the left wing of the triptych, the portrait of the imp on the right wing, and the portrait of the queen on the centrepiece of the triptych.

How was the process of creating these portraits for you? What are their messages? Jot them down in your journal. How can you benefit from each aspect of your psyche in turn? Write down your answer.

Activity n. 2

This time, you will need your triptych from the previous activity, your journal, and pen. You will need a minimum of ten minutes, or longer, for this process.

Open your triptych and put it in front of you. Interview each of the three characters, by asking each one the following questions:

What is your name?
How are you connected to my current circumstances?
What is your message for me at this time? What should I know?
What is your gift or challenge for me now?

As you answer the questions, give yourself time to shift into these aspects of yourself, by using your non-dominant hand and by writing down what comes first, without editing, even if what you receive may seem absurd or irrelevant.

Take your time with this process. At the end, drink some water, breathe deeply, and put your journal aside. Re-read the "interviews" a day or two later. What did you find out? Is there anything striking or surprising for you? Reflect on your current circumstances, and see if there are any connecting dots, as you re-read the "interviews".

Activity n. 3

Select three words that rhyme at rhymer.com and write a riddle in 4 lines. The first three lines should rhyme, whereas the last one has to be an open question. Here is an example:

It was a cold winter night
Without any moon light
Suddenly came a white knight.
Who was he?

Let the question you come up with guide and stimulate your imagination. When your riddle is ready, use it to jumpstart your writing; journal on it or let it unfold as a short story or little tale of your own. Have fun with it!

Chapter Six

The Golden Bird

Long ago, there was a king who had a beautiful orchard. He loved his fruit trees, especially the apple tree in the centre of the garden, because it bore wonderful, tasty, and shiny apples. The king was so jealous of his apples that he would have someone count all the gathered apples at the beginning and at the end of the day.

Once, it happened that by the end of the day, three apples went missing. The king was furious and appointed his gardener as guardian of the apple tree. After a few days, it was decided that the gardener's first son should find out what had happened and who had taken the apples. However, the young man fell asleep and missed the chance to discover who the thief was. The same happened to the gardener's second son. Then, the gardener's third son decided to try, even if his father wasn't willing to let him try, from fear that something bad should befall him; but the son was so determined that he finally let him try.

The youngster stayed awake well past midnight, when he saw a magnificent golden bird fly into the garden and steal an apple with its beak. The boy shot an arrow but could not hit the bird, which only dropped a feather from its tail. Thus, the boy took it and the day after he went to report to his royal highness the king what had happened in the orchard and produced the golden feather of the wondrous bird.

All the wise men of the kingdom inspected the feather and declared it was worth more than all the riches hoarded in the realm. On hearing that, the king decided he should have the whole golden bird. Thus, the gardener's first son set out on his quest for the golden bird and before long he crossed a forest. There he met a fox and he wanted to kill it, but the fox was no ordinary fox. In fact, it was a talking fox and it beseeched the young man not to kill it, for it would give him good advice.

The fox said: "When you get out of the forest, you will come to a village. There you will see two inns opposite each other. One is merry and full of comforts; the other is solitary and shabby. Do not be allured by the former; go straight to the latter and spend the night there, so that you can wake up refreshed for your quest."

The young man listened to the fox all very well, but then he thought: "What can a fox such as this know?" and he shot an arrow and missed the fox, which disappeared into the thick of the forest.

When he arrived at the village, sure enough the young man thought: "I should be very silly to pass by this happy inn" and in he went without further thoughts. There he joined the other clients, made merry, forgot all about the golden bird and about his country too. He never went back to the king's palace, so that, after a while, his second brother decided to try his luck and set off to find the golden bird, but the same events happened to him. He didn't mind the advice of the fox and went into the merry inn and forgot all about the golden bird and about his country too.

Now, the third brother, the youngest of all, wanted to go on the quest for the golden bird, and maybe he would be able to find out about his brothers too. His father, the gardener, let him go but unwillingly, for he was very fond of him.

When the boy got into the forest and met the fox, he was very grateful for its advice. This is what happened: the youngster sat on the fox's tail and the fox instructed him, and transported him to a great castle, where he was to find the golden bird. He should pass the snoring guards, enter the castle and once in the golden bird's chamber, he should take it with its wooden cage, and not attempt to put it in the golden cage nearby, lest he should regret it.

All went exactly as the fox had advised, except that the youngster could not resist taking the bird out of the wooden cage. He tried to put it into the golden one but the golden bird shrieked so loud that the guards awoke and took him to the king, who sentenced him to death. However, he could have the bird if he was able to get the golden horse which lived in another kingdom and lead it to the king's court. Having no choice, he set out on his quest. So it was that the fox showed up again and said: "Can you see what happened because you didn't listen to me? However, I will counsel you again, so that you can find the golden horse."

So, the youngster was instructed again and transported to another castle on the fox's tail. He went into the stables and saw the golden horse, while the groom was asleep, but again, instead of saddling it with the old leather saddle, he took the golden one next to the groom's head. At that, the groom woke up, and again he was convicted and brought before the king of that realm.

"Very well"—said the king—"you will die for this, unless you can bring me the princess that lives in the neighbouring realm."

At that, the youngster's spirits sank really low. How would he accomplish all of that? Once again, he set out and met the fox.

"Why did you not listen to me?"—it rebuked him—"however, I will counsel you again."

So it was that the youngster travelled on the fox's tail again and once he reached the new castle, he went in and kissed the princess, who agreed to let him lead her away. However, she entreated him to let her take leave from her parents. At first, he refused to let her go, as the fox had instructed, but since she wept a lot, he finally gave in. Once again, he was found out and sentenced to death, unless he could remove the huge hill standing in front of the king's window. If he could do that, he could have the princess.

The youngster was very dejected, for the hill was huge indeed. How was he to accomplish that? He sat down a little while to take stock of his misadventures and regretted not having listened to the fox's good advice. He then started digging. Soon enough, the fox showed up.

"Why didn't you listen to me?"

It was evening and there was no way the youngster could remove the hill. The fox said:

"Now, go to sleep! I will work for you."

In the morning, the hill was no longer there, so the youngster went to the king and asked for the princess, full of happiness. The king kept his word and off they went. Then the fox came and said:

"We will have all three: the princess, the horse, and the bird, if you would only listen to me!"

"That would be wonderful, but how can you do it?" said the youngster.

The fox instructed him carefully:

"When you come to the king who asks for the beautiful princess, say, 'Here she is!' He will joyfully give you the golden horse, which you will mount. Stretch out your hand to take leave of them but shake hands with the princess only at last: lift her on the horse and gallop away as fast as you can."

This time, the youngster did as the fox had instructed and all went well. Then the fox said:

"When you reach the castle where the golden bird is, wait for the king to bring the bird out of the castle, and when he arrives, stay on the horse, saying that you want to check if it is the true golden bird. Once you get it, ride away."

And it all happened so. The youngster carried off the princess, the horse, and the bird. Now, the fox asked him to cut off his head and feet, but the youngster refused to do it. Yet the fox instructed him once again:

"On your way back, be careful not to ransom anyone from the gallows, and do not sit by any river."

This piece of advice seemed simple enough for the youngster to follow, but as he rode, he came to the village where his brothers had stayed. Since they had become robbers, they were sentenced to the gallows, unless someone paid for their ransom. The youngster did not think twice and ransomed them at once. On their way home, they came to a wood, and his brothers told him:

"Let us rest by the river, so that we can eat and drink."

The youngster forgot the fox's advice and complied, but once near the river, his brothers took him from behind and threw him into the river bed. Then, they took the princess, the horse, and the bird and went home to the king, boasting that they had won everything for him. Then, the king gave a great feast, but the horse would not eat, the bird would not sing and the princess could not stop weeping.

Meanwhile, the god youngster had fallen to the bottom of the dry river, and both his bones and spirit were broken. He could not get out by himself. The fox came once again and scolded him bitterly for not listening to him. Then it offered its tail to haul the youngster out of the river. Then, he advised the youngster that he should disguise himself as a beggar, for his brothers had the intention to kill him. He did as the fox had advised. Once he got into the castle, the horse started eating again, the bird sang, and the princess stopped weeping. Then, he came before the king and revealed his identity and his brothers' plots against him.

The eldest brothers were punished and everyone rejoiced. The youngster and the princess were reunited and at the king's death, they became the new king and queen.

A long time after, while walking in the wood, the king met the fox again. It entreated him to kill it. This time, he did as the fox asked, cutting off its head and feet. At once, the fox turned into a man, who was no other than the queen's brother, who had been missing for many years. There were great celebrations all over the kingdom. The young queen rejoiced to see her brother again.

Themes and Motifs

The tale belongs to the Brothers Grimm's 1812 collection. It is full of symbolism and motifs that can be read on different levels of meaning. It is a tale full of wisdom.

The king is the master of the orchard and holds the apple tree at its centre very dear. The king is the ruler, the principle of authority and power. The apple tree in the garden or orchard is reminiscent of the garden of Eden, Avalon—the island of the apples—and other myths from around the world. The apples symbolise attainment of life, nourishment, perfection, beauty. Thus, it is fit that a special bird, such as the golden bird, should feed itself on the royal apples. The bird is special as it has golden feathers, reminding us of the precious metal and also the supreme substance of spiritual attainment and truth.

The gardener is the orchard's caretaker and has three sons that set out on the quest to find the golden bird. The first two fall asleep and do not see the golden bird in the garden, but the youngest one catches a glimpse of it, and he even obtains one of his precious feathers.

The youngest son is traditionally associated with naiveté and innocence. His father fears something bad could happen to him and only reluctantly does he let him try to guard the apple tree at night. The feather the youngster obtains is the key to identify the golden bird and to have the wise men of the kingdom determine that the feather alone is already worth more than all the riches in the kingdom. The youngster is the holy fool, who then sets out on the quest to find the golden bird, and through trials and errors, and because of his pure heart, he ends up gaining much more than foreseen.

The two elder sons could be considered as the embodiments of complexes in the psyche, made up of emotions, ideas, memories, and prejudices developed through experiences and interpretations that have not been well integrated in the psyche. Thus, it stands to reason that the healthy ego, symbolised by the youngest brother, should set out in their wake, but should avoid the first pitfall they encounter, which arrests their progress and makes them forget their quest, or higher purpose. In fact, they prefer the merry, glittery inn to the simple one, thus being distracted from the quest for the golden bird.

The youngest brother, instead, chooses the simple inn, where he sleeps and awakens refreshed for the quest. Thus, the inns stand for the ways of the world and its distractions, and the focus and single-mindedness necessary to undertake the quest, respectively.

The youngest brother has good will and focus, innocence and good nature on his side, so he is the one destined to achieve the quest. However, he is young and inexperienced, so he commits mistakes that lead him to complications and three death sentences, unless he can bring a new, more precious item to each offended king. This leads him to three different castles and three quests nested one within the other. Thus, the complications drive him deeper and forward to an ever-higher goal. Since he represents the healthy ego, blessed but in need of refinement, he falls prey to illusions and misjudgement. He in fact, reckons that the golden bird has to be put in a golden cage, not in an ordinary, wooden one, and the horse has to have a special golden saddle, instead of the old leather one. This signifies our ego's need for special status, acknowledgement, and validation, but it is born, developed, and nurtured in the inner silence of the psyche.

The three castles can represent sacred enclosures, places of protection that hold treasure, which the ego has to learn to obtain even through a degree of trickery, that is, psychological savviness that only comes through experience.

The talking fox that gives the good-natured youngster precious advice represents sound reason united to intuition. The prodigious fox's tail, capable of transporting the youngster to the castles as fast as the wind, represents the perfect alinement to intuition and intuitive knowledge that can lead us to all the right places we need to "visit" in our lives.

It is only reasonable that the youngster should not attempt to change the cage and the saddle, lest he should wake up the guards and the groom. Yet, as so often happens in life, he falls into the trap, the temptation of knowing or doing better, and as a consequence he is in trouble. Yet, the fox, or intuitive reason, comes to his aid repeatedly, and in the end, he is able to turn his errors into a triple achievement, by gaining not only the golden bird, but also the golden horse and the princess.

The youngster that wakes up the groom and the guards in his attempt at overachieving can represent the defences of the ego waking up and preventing the transformation of the ego into the proper, individuated self.

The three increasingly precious prizes—the golden bird, the horse, and the princess—embody higher mind, spirit, and soul. All these gifts need to be gained through tests and trials, and need to be united for the psyche to become whole. However, there is the huge hill of karma to be cleared, before we are allowed to achieve the high prize of spiritual awakening and attainment.

It is only through the action of intuitive reason, where our attempts at cleverness are asleep (as the youngster goes to sleep and the fox removes the hill for him) that we can integrate our feelings, reason, intuition, spirit and soul into one, the true self. On our way to do so, we must still face the inferior instincts and the attachments we may have, symbolised by the plot of the eldest brothers against the youngest, after he has ransomed them from the gallows.

Despite knowing better, we often fall because of our instincts, attachments, and old stories that don't serve us well in our quest for individuation. The fast horse represents the principle of untamed spirit; the beautiful princess represents the soul, led by love and devotion.

When the bird, the horse, and the princess are taken over and claimed by the eldest brothers through deceit, despite the mundane celebrations of the court, they refuse to eat, sing, and smile. This signifies the hollowness of the mundane that usurps the rights of our innermost self, the only one capable and destined to achieve the spiritual quest, because it is the only one that is driven by the sense of its unique purpose and vocation in this life.

The princess is weeping because she first wants to take leave from her parents, signifying the attachments that the soul has to release too in order to progress. Then, she cries again, till the worthy youngster comes and is recognized. They are reunited by the king: this is a symbol of the sacred marriage of the two aspects of the psyche, the feminine and the masculine, which become lawful heirs to the throne of the kingdom.

Disguised as a humble beggar, the youngster comes to court, and as soon as he enters the castle, he is recognised by the bird, horse, and princess—mind, spirit, and soul. Long after the recognition of the self and the sacred inner marriage of opposites, the new king goes walking in the wood.

It is beautiful that he goes simply walking, not hunting, on his own, thus pointing to the need for the self to cultivate its connection to itself and through nature through solitude and contemplation. There he meets his old friend, the fox, again. When the fox implores him to be killed, the young king follows through and the fox turns out to be his brother-in-law, who had been missing for years.

This can symbolise the need for continual renewal of consciousness; even the intuitive reason has to be regenerated and become more of itself through a complete metamorphosis: fully human in the highest possible sense. At this point, the young king (the self) not only has seen the reunion of spirit and soul, but also integrates a sense of communal bond, which transcends blood ties (his eldest brothers that betrayed him) to reach out towards elective affinity and the reunion with his soul family (represented by his brother-in-law).

This last part, where the young king, now more mature, goes out into the wood on his own for a walk, is remarkable. While in most folk and fairy tales the king goes hunting into the wood and is followed by a big retinue of huntsmen and companions, here the king honours his need for solitude and contemplation. In so doing, he meets his old friend, the fox, again, far from the noise of the world, mundane duties and responsibilities. The king is wise, in that he communes with himself and with nature. Nature that, in the form of a fox, has served him so well, now asks to be liberated in its own turn. It asks to be freed from the binds of necessity. And the young king frees it into a new, higher form, a human being. This symbolises a new bond between the self and a special community of kindred souls.

The king has already fulfilled his duties as a just and compassionate ruler towards his subjects. Now, he finds a deeper, nourishing connection with his brother-in-law: true friendship and reciprocal support on the ways of life.

'The Golden Bird' is such a beautiful, multi-layered metaphor for the experience of initiation into self-hood and the quest many are called to, some answer to, and only a few achieve. This is an encouraging, hopeful tale for, no matter how often we fall, we can get back on track, if our motivations are pure and authentic. We can fall prey to illusions, attachments, greed and the like, but as long as we keep on following the golden thread at the core of our lives, we can achieve our personal quests.

Self-denial, courage, honesty, humility, focus, good will, and trust in intuition and reason can lead us a good stretch of the way. Then, our right aspiration opens a serendipitous space that can be filled with the required action, proper thought, and intentional feeling.

The process of self-refinement is ongoing; it can take a very long time, yet, it is totally worthwhile, the story says. We can encounter the numinous within ourselves; in the process of interacting with the world and with our inner worlds, we also come to know ourselves and to become kings and queens of our own life domains, able to make choices, take intentional actions and take responsibilities for them, while also being blessed with the company of few like-minded companions.

Creative Process Activities

Activity n. 1: Write a Stoku

For this activity, you will need your pen and journal. "Stoku" is a word invented by accomplished Nigerian writer Ben Okri. It is a union of story and haiku. It involves writing a haiku as a set-up, or springboard for the following little story, or tale. A haiku, as you may be aware, is a short Japanese poem made up of three lines of five, seven, and five syllables, respectively. In English, each syllable can be counted by taking into consideration the stress or beats falling on words, which can be strong or weak. Where does your voice linger more strongly when pronouncing a word? That counts as a strong beat.

For example: "The colourful wood" is a five-syllable line with two strong beats ("co-" and "wood") and three weak beats ("the", "-lour", "-ful").

The colourful wood (5 syllables)
bursts into the twilight air (7 syllables)
with frenzied dead leaves (5 syllables)

If you don't want to count the syllable, just make sure that each of the three lines of your haiku is the shortest phrase or sentence you can pronounce in one breath.

Let us proceed to the steps for you to follow to write a stoku:

Breathe in and out slowly, at least three times. Sit with your feet touching firmly the ground and stretch your arms, neck, and shoulders.

Select a moment in the fairy tale that resonated with you.

Write a haiku about it, following the steps outlined above.

Use the haiku as a set-up, or prompt to write a new tale about whatever comes: let your imagination lead you.

Write as much or as little as you need to, without stopping to edit.

After a few hours, or one or two days, go back and re-read what you wrote. Edit if you need to.

Most of all, relax and let your tale speak to you: what comes to mind? What do you need right now? What is your tale telling you? Journal your answers.

Activity n. 2: Drawing and Dialogue

Re-read the fairy tale, then gather your journal, pens, crayons, pencil, and blank paper sheets. On the blank paper, draw a sketch of each of the settings of the fairy tale. You may want to focus on the following: the apple garden; the castle where the golden bird is; the stables where the horse is; the castle where the princess lives; the wood.

Draw the sketches quickly at first, to retain your own impressions of them. Once finished, add as many details as you want. Add colour, texture, differentiate the traits and contours of the objects: add the wooden and the golden cages; the apple tree, the golden bird, and its golden feather; the horse and the saddles; the princess, and the fox in their respective settings.

When you are ready, take out your journal and start a dialogue with the above-mentioned objects. For example, you may start with a kind of ritual invitation, such as: "I invite the wise fox to come forward. Come, and speak to me, please!"

Then, go on writing in the form of a dialogue between you and the character of the fox. Ask questions and note down the answers. Do not worry if it all sounds a bit crazy, just trust the process and write it all down in your journal. Do the same with the other objects, animals, and characters in the various settings you drew.

You can also ask questions based on how you drew some specific details. For example, if your fox looks sad, or the wooden cage is open, you can ask: "How come do you look so sad?" or "Why is your door open?"

Listen to the answers that come; do not dismiss any of them. Your task is to transcribe them faithfully in your journal. Repeat the process, till you have sifted through all the story settings.

Once you are finished, just close your journal and relax. Drink some water, go and do something altogether different. Re-read after a few days. Have fun and highlight what jumps at you as significant, bizarre or curious.

SECTION III
VOICE(S)

Chapter Seven

The Little Mermaid

Voice is unique. There is no such thing as two identical voices. Our voices are the signatures of our souls. In their timbre, range, tone, they express our unique identities. When we are able to speak up, to speak in our true voice, to express ourselves through our voices in speaking and singing, we are leaving our energetic imprints in our surroundings and in people's minds and hearts, even if apparently the articulations of voice fade away and last only for a limited time.

The fact is that all spiritual and mystical traditions around the world recognize the power of intentional speaking, devotional singing, praying, invocation, evocation, chanting, making vocal sounds, and humming.

The voice is woven through our bodies out of our vocal cords in response to vibrations produced by the incoming air we breathe and exhale. Our bodies are exquisite musical instruments capable of producing wondrous pieces of vocal art. Voice also is a portentous exploration tool, whereby the soul engages in self-contemplation, knowledge, and interaction with the surrounding world.

Our abilities to listen, hear, speak, sing, to articulate what we feel, think, sense, and learn are all connected. Voice can bring us close to the sense of the numinous, the divine. It can also liberate us, vindicate and rescue us, and give us the power to reclaim what is ours through brave self-expression.

The tales gathered in this section all deal with the fundamental power and psycho-spiritual status of the voice as soul signature. The first tale, '*The Little Mermaid*' was written by Hans Christian Andersen, a nineteenth-century Danish author. It is very popular due to countless reinterpretations, such as Disney's much debated animation movie.

The Little Mermaid

In the depths of the blue ocean, lives and thrives a whole kingdom of special creatures. In fact, the ocean is not only made of sand and water, but it is full of wonders, such as colourful or strange fish and the sea kingdom too.

The mermaids and mermen live happily for three hundred years, but since they do not possess an immortal soul, at their death they turn into sea foam. They usually lead cheerful, content lives, but there was once one of them that was melancholic and longed for life on earth. It was a little mermaid, the youngest of the six daughters of the sea king. They were lovingly raised by their grandmother, given that the sea king was a widower.

The youngest one was a thoughtful, solitary child, who did not care for parties and games with fish and sea horses as her sisters did. She tended her little garden, where she had grown flowers as red as the sunset, which she saw filtered through the waters, down there at the bottom of the ocean. She had retrieved a statue of a beautiful young boy from a shipwreck, and she adorned it daily with garland and foliage. She often sighed, when she thought or heard about life on earth from adult mermaids' accounts.

"When you are grown up, you too will be able to swim up to the surface of the ocean and see all the things you are asking about"—said her wise grandmother.

Each year, one of her sisters would turn fifteen and was allowed to swim to the surface of the ocean. Each would report what she had liked the most. One reported the beauty of sunlight at dawn, another loved the green hills and the rivers and forests of the earth, another still said that the sky was the most beautiful sight, and on and on. The little mermaid, on her part, was impatient for her turn to come and would spend a long time on her own, just imagining and pining for life on earth.

At length, her own turn arrived. The day she turned fifteen, her grandmother adorned her as the high-rank sea princess she was, but the little mermaid felt encumbered by the trappings and finery, the shells, and the pearls. She would have gladly gone without. She was so impatient with joy!

When she finally emerged from the ocean depths, the sun was setting, and soon the colours of the twilight moved her soul. She saw a big ship, where the people were feasting and celebrating. She swam near and she saw in the darkening sky of the evening that coloured flames shot from the deck of the ship. She had never seen fireworks. The crew and the guests were celebrating the young prince's birthday. They danced, sang and played sweet music. The little mermaid had never been so happy.

She had the most beautiful voice ever heard, but to human ears, it sounded like the wind and the sea. She was a harmonious dancer and sweet singer and naturally her heart would leap at the sound of music. She was most cherished by the sea king, her father, her sisters, and grandmother.

On hearing such joyful celebrations, the little mermaid desired to be able to take part in them, and when she approached the ship, she saw the young prince. He was so handsome: he had deep black eyes, and a high brow. She was smitten with love at first sight, for he looked so like the statue of the boy she had tended all her childhood. When, after midnight, the celebrations were over, and all the lights in the ship went out, and all was quiet, the little mermaid felt dejected, for she had no chance of ever partaking of human joy.

As she was absorbed in such gloomy thoughts, the sky became lit with lightning, clouds accumulated and soon thunder and tempest followed. The ship was out of control, the helmsman and the crew could not govern it to avoid the dangers of the storm. Everyone on board was in a frenzy. Soon, the ship was dismembered, planks and wooden objects were floating in the ocean and the people held tight to them to stay alive.

The little mermaid was worried for the prince and looked for him. Finally, she saw the prince fighting for his life against the high waves. He was succumbing to their power and lost consciousness. The little mermaid dove deep and retrieved the unconscious body. She held the prince's head on her bosom and swam towards the shore. She laid him down on the beach and raised his head; then she swam back into the ocean and sat on a rock, looking and waiting for somebody to find the prince she had rescued.

It now happened that she had left the prince on a holy island where some maiden dwelt in a sanctuary, where they were being educated. One came to the beach, and after a little fright she came near and, seeing the prince, she caressed his forehead. He opened his eyes and smiled feebly. Soon, the other maidens arrived and took care of him and helped him to walk inside. The little mermaid could no longer see him, and was greatly vexed by the fact he didn't know that she had rescued him from the storm.

She swam back to the depths of the ocean and refused to talk to anyone. She grew so dejected and lonely that even her beautiful garden was untended and became overgrown. Her sisters and grandmother were very worried for her. One day, the little mermaid opened her heart to one of her sisters, who had a friend who happened to know who the prince was. Thus, all the sisters came to know what the matter was and decided to emerge from the ocean with their little sister to help her find out what had been of the prince.

And they did so; but when they found the prince's castle with its majestic flight of stairs reaching out to the sea, they also learned that the king was looking for the right betrothed for his son.

The little mermaid was deeply sad. How could she ever aspire to become the prince's beloved with her long fish tail? How she wished she were human and had legs instead of a fish tail! She retreated to the bottom of the ocean sadder than ever. Despair was in her heart, and her sisters blamed themselves for the idea of finding out about the prince.

They tried in vain to persuade their little sister that their lives there at the bottom of the ocean were happy and beautiful. She grew more and more despondent, longing for a human body and an immortal soul with all her energy. She pined, and sighed, and suffered more pain than human girls, for mermaids have no tears and cannot cry. This went on for a few days, till she came to a fatal choice: she would go to the sea witch, whom anyone feared and avoided, because she was dangerous and evil. Yet, she was very, very powerful. The little mermaid was possessed with her new resolution and she told no one about her intention.

When her sisters were having a ball at court, she swam away unnoticed. She swam and swam for many leagues, till she reached a spot in the ocean where the bottom was bare and grey. Nothing grew there. There were no seaweeds, no sand, no colourful fish, or playful seahorses. The only living creatures were polyps that looked like petrified plants. They took hold of pieces and objects from ship-wrecked vessels, bones and skulls. They had even strangled a mermaid who had roamed too far.

The little mermaid was scared. Yet, she would not go back. She rolled her long hair around her head and folded her arms closely, so that the polyps that guarded the witch's abode could not hold her, and darted across them at full speed.

She finally was at the witch's door. Her heart thumped in her chest.

"I know what you want"—said a husky voice—"come inside."

The little mermaid pushed the door and saw a terrible sight: the witch sat at the very end of a dark room, with fluorescent snakes as hair, bleary eyes and sinister smile. She was surrounded by slimy little creatures, whom she called her children.

"You want to become human, to have legs instead of your fish tail."

The little mermaid nodded.

"I can do it"—said the witch—"but you can only have an immortal soul, if a man falls in love with you, and marries you. This way, you can partake of a human soul. Do you want to attempt it?"

"I will"—said the little mermaid.

"But think again"—said the witch—"you are stupid for wanting this; but you will have your way. I can prepare a potion that will give legs to your body, but you will feel pain, as if a sword tore your body in two. And when you will dance for the prince as graciously as ever a human girl could, you will feel as if you were walking on the sharp edges of a hundred knives. And you will be broken-hearted the morning after your prince marries another and your death comes. Besides, I must be paid for my potion. And it is costly. I will have your heavenly voice."

"But what will be left of me once you take away my voice?" —said the little mermaid.

"Your beautiful human form and your expressive eyes should be enough to have the prince fall in love with you. Are you afraid?"

"It shall be done!"—said the little mermaid.

"Then, put out your tongue, that I may cut it."

And it was so. The little mermaid opened her mouth and the witch cut her tongue. Now she was dumb!

The witch prepared her potion and at the end of all her stirring, she put some of the liquid in a vial. The potion looked so clear that it may well have been water, except that it was terribly powerful.

When the little mermaid left the witch's den, holding her precious vial, the polyps let her through for fear of the potion that would break their tentacles in a hundred pieces, and dissolve their bodies.

The little mermaid went back to her father's castle and looked at her sisters from afar. She was now dumb and didn't want them to know. She swam to the ocean's surface and swam to a rock in front of the shore, then she drank the potion. She felt as if her whole body were torn asunder; such a strong, deep pain went through her body that she lost her consciousness.

When she woke up, she saw the prince's beautiful eyes look at her in earnest, asking her whence she came and who she was, but she could only look back at him with her expressive, sad eyes, and since she was naked, she covered her human body with her long hair.

The prince had her led inside and she grew to be his confidante. He declared she should always be near and sleep on a cushion outside his door, but never did he think he would marry her. He called her his "little foundling" and confessed to her ears how he longed for the young woman who had saved him on the island, to whom his heart belonged ever since. Thus, the little mermaid's heart was full of sadness, because she would never be able to tell him the true story of how she had rescued him from the storm. She kept him company, and danced gracefully for him, although her feet felt cut by the sharp edges of one hundred knives, as the witch had said.

The day the king had set for the prince to meet his betrothed approached. The prince confessed to his little foundling, whose devotion he was aware of, he only intended to meet her before taking a decision, for the little mermaid knew well what was in his heart.

When the moment came, he entered a big pavilion and rejoiced in meeting his beloved, the one he presumed to have saved his life, as his betrothed. After a few months, they were married and when the celebrations were over, in the dark night, the little mermaid felt her end was coming.

As she looked out at sea, she saw her sisters beckoning from afar.

"Come"—they said—"we have given our hair to the sea witch to have you preserve your mermaid life. Take the knife emerging from the sea and kill the prince as he sleeps. This way you will be free and you will live."

She lifted the knife out of the water and went into the prince's pavilion. He was sleeping so tenderly with his head on his beloved's bosom, that she had no heart to kill him. She loved him more than ever. Instead, she kissed both the prince and the princess on their brows, went out and threw the knife into the ocean. The waves were as red as blood where it had sunk.

She stood on the deck, felt her heart was broken, and dove into the ocean, waiting to become sea foam. She figured she was being transformed into the waves, when she lost consciousness.

Then, she awakened in a strange, rarefied atmosphere and her voice was back: "Where am I?"—she asked.

"Because of your good deeds, you have been transformed into an air spirit, a sylph, and in three hundred years you may be given an immortal soul by guiding children to do good,"—the air spirits told her. And they rejoiced at her arrival among them. Later, when the prince and the princess woke up, they looked for her everywhere and were full of sorrow for their loss.

Themes and Motifs

'The Little Mermaid' is such a powerful tale that it has been object of different emotional reactions ever since it was published.

In 1913, a statue of the little mermaid was erected on a rock emerging from the sea, close to the shore in Copenhagen. More recently, some feminist critics have considered the tale unfit to be told to children, especially girls, because of its treatment of the loss of voice. Indeed, voice in the tale is a powerful theme and it is considered the very seat of personal identity the little mermaid gives up in order to have a chance of being loved by the prince.

Understandably, the feminist critics see this as a supreme example of a dangerous self-sacrifice, whereby the mermaid/woman gives up her own essence, truth and self-expression—her voice—because of love for a man. However, the tale is very profound and the theme of sacrificing one's own voice is deep and true-to-life, for often in life, countless people, both women and men, have done so because of the desire to attain something which, at the time of their sacrifice, feels more precious to them than self-expression.

The tale highlights how the mermaid is both an introvert, thoughtful and solitary creature, and restless because of a desire she cannot attain, because it is beyond her own fate, beyond what nature has allotted her kind. Her aspiration to love a human and to have an immortal soul is seen as unnatural by her sisters. Yet, she loves human beings so deeply that she never wants to go back to the bottom of the ocean.

Indeed, the little mermaid herself could be seen as a symbol of redemption and transformation through self-sacrifice, denial and pain, which is not particularly appreciated by feminist critics. On the other hand, we can also consider her as the symbol of the emancipation of the self through the dismantling of the ego. While it is not for her to attain her desired human love, she is rewarded at the end with a further transformation. Therefore, it seems to me that the major themes of the tale are change and voice.

Change is ever present, it is a constant and it teaches both joy and sorrow, and ultimately some measure of equanimity and compassion. Voice can be silenced, repressed, renounced even. In the end, though, the little mermaid regains her own voice because of her courage and love. She decides to throw the knife back into the ocean, instead of killing the man she loves to regain her former status of mermaid and, in doing so, she is given a third possibility and a real chance to attain an immortal soul. Because of this unfoldment, I do not agree with the criticisms levelled at the tale.

Learning about the mermaid's reward at the end of the story allows us to work out some important implications. The little mermaid does not throw away her voice casually; she is all too aware of what is giving up in doing so. In fact, she asks the sea witch what will be left of her, once her voice is no longer there.

In giving up her most precious gift, she goes through trial after trial and finally, her heart is broken. Yet, she also has the power and fortitude of love on her side. Depending on the given circumstances, renouncing one's voice can be an act of courage and love, or an act of acquiescence. In the case of the little mermaid, her love is so complete that she is shaped by it. Her identity loses the power of voice, it also gains the depth of character bestowed by authentic love and courage. If she had preserved her harmonious voice, she would never have experienced being a human being.

The sea witch can be considered as a symbol of the realm of abjection that holds what we most fear and loathe, what repels us down to our very core because it bears witness to a liminal place where the sense of one own's identity is dissolved and mingled with the sense and experience of Otherness. Thus, in descending to this realm where nothing grows but all feeds off wrecks and corpses, the little mermaid undergoes the sharpest, most poignant initiation. Like Inanna descending to the underworld, the little mermaid casts off her most distinctive characteristics: her voice and her beautiful fishtail; the former as payment to the abject realm itself; the latter as a pawn and a price of admission to the human realm.

The abject is represented by the sea witch as an uncanny, disgusting, powerful creature outside the order of both the sea kingdom and the human kingdom; thus, because her realm is liminal and beyond order and rules, it holds the huge power of death and transformation. It could be argued that the sea-witch, representative of the negative mother archetype, can be seen as swallowing up and destroying all of life, as the violent, ferocious aspect of nature cast out into a barren, grey dimension. Yet, from the abject and abysmal the mermaid obtains a clear, crystal-like potion with the power of transforming her into a woman and the ability to live in another experiential plane, that of the earth.

The little mermaid comes to know three realms in her life: water, earth and air, that is the realm of the unconscious, the realm of the conscious and of earthly love, and the realm of the ideal, the superconscious. Her good deeds are more than moral deeds, they are absolute acts of rebellion in the name of a love that transcends the boundaries between the human and the other-than-human realms.

Her love is as deep as the ocean whence she comes, as warm and nurturing as the earth she treads on when she embraces her human life, as pure as the ethereal kingdom of the air sprites. The play with the elements is an important symbolic factor in the tale. In the end, it is implied that because of all of that, she will be infused with an immortal soul—spiritual fire—the last element to be added for alchemical transmutation. It seems to me that this tale is about nothing less than the birth of the soul.

If we consider the earth as "the Vale of soul-making", the little mermaid's transformations can be read as stages in the psyche's initiation process, whereby it proceeds from the unconscious to the earthly lessons of pain, joy, love, to the ideal realm of superior consciousness and the transpersonal, to the attainment of spiritual heights and to spiritual integration.

It is an unpopular psychological truth that we cannot have everything we want and, least of all, all at once. Thus, the little mermaid giving up her distinctive voice hints at the totalising experience of devotion and unselfish love. We are called to give up what is seemingly most important for our sense of identity to attain our unique quest, which is always based on a form of love, at its most essential core.

The quest may turn out differently from what we hope or expect, as it is the case with the little mermaid and as it happens most of the time in life, because we make our paths as we live. The distinctiveness of our path is indeed the fact that we carve it into being as we go along, through our choices and actions. Paradoxically, we may find out at the next bend on our road that we have given up is not lost but transposed and regained at another level of consciousness, as it is symbolised by the situation of the little mermaid speaking again in the air kingdom.

Another remarkable theme in the tale is that of dancing lightly through life and its sorrows, despite or even because of them. The little mermaid chooses the path of awakening through pain. We are told she dances beautifully and lightly for the prince, while she feels the pain of one hundred sharp-edged knives cutting her feet. And for all her pain, she dances on. She loves life, she loves the earth, humans, the prince, but she unknowingly has to pursue her way of devotion till a breakthrough happens. The moment she goes to the sea witch and she is told all she will go through, she chooses a form of love asceticism. Her trials remind us of freedom of choice, which does not mean that we can do, have or be whatever we want, but that we can pursue the choice of becoming who we truly are from the beginning—or we may not. In fact, we are told that the little mermaid as a child is solitary, contemplative, thoughtful and full of longing to know the earth. We are also told that she tends a garden with a statue of a little boy that looks like the prince she will later meet.

The statue is a symbol of some mysterious aspiration imprinted in the individual soul from the start, as a mark and a sign of a unique, specific destiny and calling in life. Indeed, it would be so vitally important for everyone to notice the signs of their unique calling and vocation in life, instead of running endlessly on the treadmill of widespread illusions and lies.

This sense of finding, acknowledging, and pursuing our own destiny seems to be lost in much of our modern—or traditional—patriarchal cultures. When institutions of various kinds stifle the soul, by putting individuals into boxes according to artificial, soulless categories and requirements, we lose our threads, the sense of our precious destiny and calling. So many people, both young and old, go through life numbed, disoriented, and hopeless they do not hold the thread of their own vocations in life. As the beautiful, revelatory lines by William Stafford state in 'The Way It Is', we must never let go of our thread, no matter what happens in our lives.

Creative Process Activities

Activity n. 1: Write a Sequel

For this activity you will only need your journal and a pen.

Ground yourself through the practising of breathing in and out and focusing on your breath. Practise for at least two minutes. If your attention wanders, just bring it back to your breath. Make sure you are sitting with a straight back and feet firmly laid on the ground. Choose a comfortable chair, better if it can support your back. Close your eyes and focus on inhaling, holding, and exhaling. Set an alarm clock to help keep you focused.

When you are finished, re-read the fairy tale with attention, savouring its scenes and developments. Then sit down with your journal and pen and imagine how the mermaid's new life as a sylph could unfold: write your own sequel to *'The Little Mermaid'*.

Enjoy the imaginative process and let your pen move in a flow, without stopping to edit. Capture all the first ideas you have and see where they lead you. Explore, be open, do not judge yourself, your process or the story that is unfolding for you.

Activity n. 2: Exploring Silence

Choose a calm day, when you can be on your own most of the time. Devote yourself to silence as an exploratory practice. Avoid speaking or singing, be as still as you can. You can practise solitary sports, such as jogging, but avoid social media, TV, radio, cinema, Internet, email and even reading and writing.

If you cannot dedicate a whole day to the practice of silence, go for a few hours: even two hours will suffice, provided you stick to the guidelines. Consider silence as a gift you give yourself to observe things, events, emotions and feelings closely. Practise being in the moment, by letting go of judgement and criticism. The only details you can take in and write down, if you wish to do so, are factual or precise observations: textures, colours, smells, sights, tastes. This is not a simple practice to carry out but if you stick to it, you will reap the rewards of enhanced presence and mental clarity, as well as relaxation.

Activity n. 3: Water Dance

The tale says the little mermaid was a gracious dancer, who could move her feet with lightness and sinuous movements.

Find some water music. You can search for the sound of sea waves on YouTube or buy some ambience music inspired by the ocean and other bodies of water: rivers, streams, lakes, rain. You could even record the sound of the stormy sea, of the waves crashing against the rocky shore, of running streams, or pouring rain. Allow for at least 10 minutes of music.

When you are undisturbed, wear some loose, comfortable clothes, get rid of your shoes and play back the water music. Relax and ease your body, mind and emotions into the rhythm and flow of the water. Put the music on repeat, and let your arms move in curves and make invisible shapes, as if you were painting in the air.

When you are satisfied with the movements of your arms and upper body, start adding the movement of your legs and feet to the constant rhythm of the water. What movements can help you do so? How can you merge with the rhythm of the water? Now, focus on your upper body and arms. Keep on breathing and relax your jaws. What movements can express flow and ease? Or energy and power?

Listen to the water music carefully and adapt the movements of your body to the perceptible changes in the music. Dance for at least ten minutes—or longer—and repeat the process for at least three days in a row. Notice how you feel.

What have you learned about flow, rhythm, and power? Have you felt the power of water in your body and emotions? How? What about surrender and letting go? Write down your reflections in your journal as soon as you finish dancing, and also a few hours later. See how you feel, and if it changes after a few hours. Did you receive any beneficial effects?

Chapter Eight

The Juniper Tree

'The Juniper Tree' was collected by the Grimm brothers in their 1812 fairy tale collection. Ever since it has been quite renown despite its grim themes and motifs.

Very long ago, there were a husband and wife that loved each other dearly but were childless. The wife would spend hours sighing and wishing for a child. They were greatly vexed by their situation.

One day, the woman sat under a big juniper tree, peeling apples with a knife. As she did so, she cut her finger. It was winter and there was snow all around.

"If only I had a child as white as snow and as red as blood!" —she sighed, and went back into her house.

Winter passed; the snow melted. Spring came and the swallows flew back from the South, the first blades of grass and violets appeared in patches on the ground. Then it was summer and the fields were ablaze with golden corn. Finally, autumn came, and the mellowness of the air and the beauty of its colours were a sweet song to be lulled by. In all seasons, the woman sat under the juniper tree. Once, as she sat, she felt her heart become light and cheerful and she knew her wish was granted. Soon enough she was with child.

When the time was ripe, she gave birth to a boy as white as snow, with cheeks as red as blood. The woman, though, fell ill and asked her husband to be buried under the juniper tree, if she was to die. And so it happened: her husband was full of sorrow and grieved her for some years. In the meanwhile, the boy grew into a thoughtful, silent lad; he was sweet and obedient.

His father ended up marrying another woman, who at first was kind to the boy, but when she had her own baby girl, things started to change. The stepmother was obsessed with the fear that her girl would not inherit anything because of the boy, and became unkind to him.

When the girl was four and the boy was seven, the stepmother would constantly scold and abuse the boy with buffetings and boxes on his ears. The boy had no respite and went to school almost in rags and greatly neglected.

One afternoon, the little girl asked for an apple to her mother, but she also wanted one for her brother, who would soon come back from school. The mother was angry but told her daughter that she should wait for her brother. The mother planned to get rid of the boy there and then. So, when he came back, his little sister welcomed him and told him that their mum would give him an apple too; to which the woman gave him a terrible look and said that indeed he could have an apple. He thanked his stepmother, who said: “Go and pick one yourself in that big wooden chest.” In the meanwhile, the little girl had gone out to play.

The boy approached the open chest, and leant over to pick up his apple but as he did so, his stepmother shut the lid with a snap and cut his head off. She was very scared for fear of being found out, so once she cleaned off all the blood, she took one of her white kerchiefs and wound it round the boy’s neck. Then, she put his body upright, sitting on a chair next to the window and put an apple in his hand.

When the little girl came inside, she asked her mother if she could have another apple.

"Go ask your brother, over there."—said the mother, "and if he doesn't answer, give him a box on his ear."

So, the little girl asked the brother for the apple, but he looked so pale and his eyes were staring and dreadful. He did not answer, so the little girl gave him a box on his ear and his head fell off to the ground.

The little girl was so scared and horrified, she jumped back and cried and sobbed aloud. Her mother said:

"What is done cannot be undone! Keep your mouth shut."—and she cut the boy into pieces and made stew of his flesh. The little girl could not be consoled, and cried and cried some more. She didn't stop; when her mother served the stew to the father and he relished it so much, she cried even more and went under the table where she gathered her brother's bones that the father had been discarding. He had asked where his son was but the stepmother said he was visiting an uncle for some weeks. He cried for sadness, and then the little girl cried even more. Then she put all the bones she had gathered in her white handkerchief and made them wet with her copious tears. She went outside and buried them under the branches of the juniper tree.

As soon as she had done so, the juniper tree seemed to move and the little girl felt her heart be light and unburdened again. Then, she went inside. A mist and a smoke enveloped the juniper tree, and a flame blazed among its branches, whence a beautiful golden and green bird flew off and away into the twilight.

The little bird flew into the village and perched on the window sill of a goldsmith's workshop and sang a strange, sad song:

My mother, she killed me and made me into stew,
My father, he cried and ate me,
My little sister, she loved me best of all
and gathered my bones for the juniper tree.
Tweet, tweet—what a beautiful bird I am!

The goldsmith, who was working on a gold chain, lifted his head and said:

"How beautifully you sing! Sing that song again!"

The bird answered: "What will you give me if I sing again?"

"Here—" said the goldsmith, "take this gold chain, and sing again for me!"

The bird took the gold chain in his right claw and then sang:

My mother, she killed me and made me into stew,
My father, he cried and ate me,
My little sister, she loved me best of all
and gathered my bones for the juniper tree.
Tweet, tweet—what a beautiful bird I am!

Then, he flew away with his gold chain and after a while, he alighted on the roof of a shoemaker's workshop, who was making a beautiful pair of red shoes. The bird sang:

My mother, she killed me and made me into stew,
My father, he cried and ate me,
My little sister, she loved me best of all
and gathered my bones for the juniper tree.
Tweet, tweet—what a beautiful bird I am!

The shoemaker was so struck with the bird's beautiful singing that he too beseeched the bird to sing it again.

To that the bird replied: "What will you give me if I sing again?"

"Here—" said the shoemaker, "take these red shoes and sing again for me!"

So, the bird took the red shoes in his left claw and sang again:

My mother, she killed me and made me into stew,
My father, he cried and ate me,
My little sister, she loved me best of all

and gathered my bones for the juniper tree.
Tweet, tweet—what a beautiful bird I am!

Then, the little bird flew away to a mill, where several men were hewing a stone. He sang his song again, and as he did so, all but one man left their work. The last man asked to hear the song again and the other joined in the request.

The little man asked for the millstone in exchange for repeating the song. Then he sang:

My mother, she killed me and made me into stew,
My father, he cried and ate me,
My little sister, she loved me best of all
and gathered my bones for the juniper tree.
Tweet, tweet—what a beautiful bird I am!

Then, all the men lifted the millstone and the little bird put it hanging around his strong neck and flew away.

In the morning, it perched on the branches of the juniper tree outside the house of his family and sang again.

On hearing his song, the father came out and listened in ecstasy, then went inside and told his wife and daughter:

"Come! There's a beautiful bird singing on the juniper tree. He sings so sweetly, and the air is full of good scents!" And out he went again. The bird flew over his head and dropped the gold chain around his neck.

The father went inside and urged his wife and daughter:

"See what beautiful gold chain he has given me!"

The little girl went out and listened to the bird's song and felt very sad, but when the little bird dropped the red shoes for her, she rejoiced and went inside with a light heart.

The mother instead could not stand listening to the song and was full of anxiety. The blood in her veins was on fire and her head was bursting. When she saw the red shoes, the bird had given her daughter, she said:

"I will go out and see what he gives me! Maybe, I will feel better!"

But as soon as she put her foot out of the house, the bird dropped the millstone on her head and crash!—her body disappeared beneath the millstone, and in its place, there was only smoke.

Then, the bird turned into the boy and his father and little sister rejoiced greatly when they saw him. All together they held hands and sat under the branches of the juniper tree.

Themes and Motifs

Several writers and scholars have commented on the gruesome elements of *'The Juniper Tree'*, which make it one of the darkest tales of the Grimms. Feminists have concentrated on the suppression and erasure of women; social history scholars have focused on the social facts the tale is rooted in, such as the exclusion of daughters from the father's inheritance, while still others have observed the theme of child psychological and physical abuse, let alone murder and cannibalism.

On my part, I selected this tale and included it in the section on voice because it allows our archetypal analysis to focus on "voice" as the tool of self-expression, vindication and truthfulness. Thus, taking each element in the tale as embodying both internal and external dynamics allows us to consider characters in folk and fairy tales as symbolising aspects of the individual psychological make-up that also get mirrored in external life circumstances through projection, prejudice, and assumption, anticipation and expectation.

'The Juniper Tree' is a tale rich in symbolical motifs.

At the beginning, a mother is peeling apples under a juniper tree, and as she cuts her finger she wishes for a son as red as blood and as white as snow. Here we have a cluster of motifs that we need to unpack. The mother symbolises the generative aspect of the psyche, as well as physical fertility. She is peeling apples, which are symbols of attainment, creativity and fertility. The blood and its red colour signify vital energy, spirit and force, as well as a phase of alchemical transformation, called "rubedo".

White is the other colour that appears in the alchemical process, together with black, yellow, and gold. White symbolises the stage of "albedo", as well as innocence and purity.

In alchemy, there are seven different stages giving birth to the following states or conditions:

Nigredo (blackness)
Albedo (whiteness)
Citrinitas (yellowness)
Rubedo (redness)
Gold (final result)

In analytical psychology, the first condition, "nigredo" corresponds to the stage of decomposition or putrefaction, psychologically known as "the dark night of the soul", where the shadow is met.

Subsequently, the individual progresses towards "albedo" and the descent into the unconscious is illuminated from above. In this second condition, "the prima materia" of consciousness, its raw content, is purified.

The third condition is citrinitas, when the solar aspect of the psyche emerges and the lunar aspect recedes.

Rubedo is the fourth condition, whereby the whole process of psychic transmutation is integrated, before returning into the world.

The final result is the achievement of the philosopher's stone, which Jung identified as a symbol of successful individuation. Gold is the colour associated with this achievement. Thus, each condition is associated to an archetype in the individual's psychic set up:

Nigredo is about meeting our Shadow, the rejected aspects of the self;

Albedo is about getting acquainted with the Anima (for men) and Animus (for women) archetypes, intended as ideal psychic images of the opposite sex, as it is about clarification, purification and illumination;

Citrinitas is about the archetype of the old wise man or woman, which is characterised by wisdom and sound judgement and ushers in the stage of rubedo.

Rubedo, the final condition, is the union of opposites, the integration of the self. Thus, it is about the Self archetype, whereby the individual is successfully formed, finally integrated and whole. The result of this process is the gold philosopher's stone.

This brief overview is useful to understand the development of the story further.

The juniper tree that grants the woman's wish to be a mother is no ordinary tree. It is about spirit companionship, the sense of belonging to an ancestral lineage, the natural embodiment of guardianship and protection. When the mother is dying, she asks to be buried under the juniper tree, meaning returning to the unbroken, life-giving line of the other-than-human ancestors.

The boy who is red and white symbolises the two alchemical processes of albedo and rubedo. However, in order for the psyche to be reborn and transmuted into the self, it has to go through nigredo at first. This is when the stepmother appears to make life hard for the boy, and finally to kill and dismember him.

The stepmother, the psychic predator, makes stew of the boy's body, symbolising the extreme pain and loss of identity, an erasure of one's sense of self. The father eating his son's flesh, thus incorporating him, is not only a reference to the practice of cannibalism—ritual or otherwise—but also a practice of assimilation and consubstantiality between father and son, being made of the same substance, quite literally. The father archetype and the child archetype coalesce in this motif.

The sister, who loves the boy "best of all", gathers his bones, which traditionally are associated with life force and the ability to bring someone back to life in countless traditional stories. Thus, the bones are the symbol of what is immortal, what endures and does not die. The little sister wets them with her tears, meaning love and devotion that feed life and in the cult of dead ancestors and relatives honouring and nourishing their memory.

Psychologically, the little sister gathering bones in her white kerchief and burying them under the juniper tree symbolises the ability of the psyche to take care of itself nursing and ministering healing to itself, going through loss, grief, rest and regeneration, also by seeking contact with the unbroken line of ancestors and/or a sense of rootedness in the natural world.

Soon enough, what comes out of the juniper tree is mist, a flame in the mist and a golden bird soaring from the flame. The bird has been associated with the soul, a symbol of resurrection and transmutation in traditional cultures all over the world. The bird's song is the song of the soul expressing both sorrow and beauty. Indeed, the deep pain of the soul is conveyed through and turned into beauty. Here, the strange, sorrowful song of the bird that entices the listener into bestowing gifts in exchange is a profound reflection on what it means to have and use our voices in the world as an expression of our souls and our experiences, and to ask for justice.

The actions of the bird with the golden feathers refer to the citrinitas stage, whereby the wisdom and judgement of the soul work towards solving karmic knots and reaching a resolution. In this respect, the millstone is the very opposite of the philosopher's stone. It is an instrument of death and retributive justice. When karma is solved, the bird can finally turn back into human form, the boy is brought back to life, although this time all the stages of individuation have been gone through and all the aspects of the psyche are integrated.

It is noteworthy that the beautiful song and voice of the bird also are the instruments of justice: beauty, creativity and self-expression can indeed bring about recognition of the truth, and thus facilitate justice, they can also move the listeners into support mode and thus facilitate change in the world. The gifts the bird obtains together with the millstone are a gold chain for the father and a pair of red shoes for the little sister. Both these gifts are described as capable of bringing mirth and joy to the receivers, whereas the millstone flattens down the stepmother's body that literally vanishes into smoke. It is interesting to look at the three ways death is depicted in the tale: when the boy's mother dies, she is buried under the juniper tree, thus living on in the body of the earth and the roots of the tree, as well as in its spirit, merging with the protective spirits of the ancestors and guardians; when the boy dies, it is through deceit and murder, and dismemberment, a symbolic initiation through dissolution; when the stepmother dies, she literally is annihilated and fades into nothingness, as a result of her misdeeds.

In the depiction of the states and conditions the various characters are subjected to, there is an interplay of the horizontal and vertical spatial dimensions. For example, the boy turns into a creature of the sky, thus is soul ascends and he is resurrected into earthly life; his mother descends into the earth and lives on in the standing tree, branches and roots; the boy/bird bestows gifts to his father and little sister from above, and the stepmother is literally flattened out, horizontally annihilated. From a symbolic point of view, her death is lost in the horizontal dimension, while all other characters' actions involve the vertical dimensions, which imply movement and evolution of the soul.

Creative Process Activities

Activity n. 1: Enacting an Alchemical Ritual With Paper

For this activity you will need the following items: coloured paper sheets (black, white, yellow, red), coloured pens, markers, crayons, watercolour paints and brushes, water jar, a bowl for the ashes, scissors, your journal, a candle, matches.

Set the scene: put on some relaxing music, breathe, and light an energising essential oil, such as bergamot, lemongrass, or cinnamon. Light a candle, settle into your body and close your eyes. Think about a time of your life when you experienced adversity; recall the details to mind. Then, remember the process that allowed you to break on through to the other side stronger and more self-aware; then, remember how your wits, wisdom and rationality helped you to make sense of and digest your experience. Finally, consider what you have learnt from the experience and how you have become the person you are today. Take your time. Don't rush. When you are ready, open your eyes and journal about all of the above.

Then, pick the black sheet and consider the painful experience, the sorrow, loss and grief. Make a mark of a symbol for that time with the white crayon. Then, crumple the paper into a ball and hold it in your left hand. Focus on releasing all the past suffering and then burn the paper ball.

Then, pick the white paper and use watercolour. Paint and use water: a stream, rain, a lake, a river, etc. Let the colour be fluid and transparent. Then hold the paper and let the paint run throughout the sheet in all directions. Remember how your trials clarified your mind and cleansed your emotions. Let the colour spread throughout the sheet. Let it dry for a while. When, it is ready, fold it at least four times and hold it in your right hand. Burn it into the candle flame.

Next, take the yellow paper and draw a big sun in the centre. Remember your growth and doodle symbols inside the contour of the sun. Then, breathe deeply, hold it with both hands and burn it too.

Finally, pick the red sheet and draw a winged heart. Write one word, phrase or sentence to synthesise your learning and transformation leading to the present moment. When you are ready, hold it into the flame and release it too.

Now close your eyes and visualise all your body filled with liquid gold from the top of your head to the soles and toes of your feet, and beyond, into the roots going down into the earth and antennae going up from your head into the sky. You are the vessel and the very stuff of transmutation. You are, metaphorically speaking, pure gold. Breathe deeply in and out and when you feel ready write any insights and/or thoughts in your journal. Sniff out the candle and dispose of the ashes in the garden, or in a park, or field.

Activity n. 2: Compose and Sing Your Soul Song

You will need pens, your journal, a recorder, and at least one musical instrument, as simple or as complex as you like, or you can build your own with simple materials, such as plastic cutlery, glasses and dishes, sticks, glass mini-bells, etc.

Think about the whole alchemical process and ask yourself what symbol resonates with your soul essence and experience. Once an image, a sound, a feeling or a sensation comes forth, observe it closely and ask:

What do you look like?
What do you taste like?
What do you smell like?
What do you sound like?
What do you feel like?

Take the time to write all the answers in your journal. Free write. Do not stop to edit.

Once you have put on paper as much detail as you can, turn a new page and write a title for what will become your song. Let the title and the refrain emerge first, starting from your soul symbol. Then, fill up the body of the song with more details from your journal. Tweak the song till it feels right and then start singing, trying out different rhythms and tunes. If you need to, accompany your voice with a musical instrument. Have fun, let it be an exploration process. Let your voice rise and fall, modulate it according to the different emotions your song intends to convey. Likewise, experiment with music: drum, stomp your foot, shout and vocalise, or ring a crystal bell, or any other resounding object. Explore and take notes along the way. When you are satisfied, record your song as you perform it for yourself. This is your soul song. Keep it sacred.

Activity n.3: Empower Your Voice!

For this activity, you will need your pen and journal, magazines, paper, or cardboard, and scissors.

Have you always had the strength and courage to speak up for yourself? Why/Why not? Or what was/is in your way? What would you need to feel confident and capable of speaking up? Write in your journal about these questions.

Then, cut out the shape of a bird from a magazine, paper sheet, or cardboard base and decorate it to your content. On the other side of the bird shape, write down words of empowerment regarding your voice ad its power of self-expression by tapping into your past and present, or by vividly imagining future possibilities for your voice. Savour and enjoy the process!

Chapter Nine

The Six Swans

'*The Six Swans*' is a tale collected by the Brothers Grimm, but there exist hundreds of variants throughout Europe and in Asia too, revolving around the motif of the heroine's brothers turned into birds, which can be swans, ravens, rooks, jackdaws and several other kinds of birds. The number of the brothers also varies: six, seven, eleven, etc.

Long time ago, there was a widower king who loved hunting in the woods alone. One day, he got lost there while pursuing a stag. He could not find his way back. He walked into the depths of the forest, till he saw a dilapidated hut. He went inside, and saw a very old woman sitting on a stool. He asked her for directions to get out of the forest.

"I can certainly help you, King"—she said—"on one condition."

The king encouraged her to speak.

"I will help you to get back to the royal palace if you marry my daughter, who is as beautiful as you could ever wish."

The king agreed but was sad, because he had a bad feeling about the matter. Besides, he already had six sons and a daughter from his previous wife, whom he had loved with all his heart.

The new queen was indeed beautiful, but her eyes and heart were as cold as stone. The king feared she would hurt his children and made sure to hide them in a castle in the forest that he himself could only find by using a ball of yarn he was given by a wise woman. So it happened that he went into the forest as often as he could, leaving the queen alone in the palace.

She began to be suspicious and bribed the servants into confessing where the king was going. Once she learnt of the king's children, she had no peace, and since she had been trained in witchcraft by her mother, she set down to sew little silken shirts. Then, she got hold of the ball of yarn and went into the forest by herself.

When she came near the castle, the six little sons ran out, thinking it was their father coming their way. As soon as she saw them, she threw the silken shirts on them and they were instantly turned into swans. Their little sister, who had not come out of the castle, had seen everything from her window. She gathered the feathers the six swans had left behind before flying away and when her father came, she told him all that had happened.

The king mourned but did not believe that the queen had done such an evil deed. Fearing for his daughter, he asked her to move back with him. The daughter beseeched her father to let her stay one more day and night in the forest castle because she was afraid of the queen and wanted to take time. Once alone, she made a small bundle for herself containing a little food and ran across the forest. She ran and ran, intending to go as far as she could from her wicked stepmother. Finally, she came to a small cottage where there were six beds and she fell asleep on one of them, since nobody seemed to live there.

At twilight, through the open windows, six swans flew inside and quickly turned into humans. It was her brothers. They rejoiced in seeing her, but told her to leave as soon as she could, for that was the cove of some thieves, who would soon come back; they were unable to protect her, for they were human only for a quarter of an hour at twilight. Then, they would turn into swans again. The sister cried and asked them if there was any way to break such a curse.

"There is"—said one of the brothers—"but the conditions are too hard! You should weave six shirts out of nettles, without ever speaking a word, crying or laughing for six years, lest the curse becomes unbreakable and eternal."

They bade her farewell and then flew away as swans.

The girl, however, was determined to rescue her brothers. She left the cottage and after a while, she came to an abandoned hut, where she started to work to break the spell. She gathered nettles at dawn and she wove them all day long. One day, she climbed up a tree and started working at her shirts up there among the branches. Soon, a neighbouring king and his hunting party came near and the dogs began to bark at the tree. Then, the king's men saw her and asked for her name and whence she came. She never answered, but dropped all her ornaments and garments in the hope of appeasing their curiosity and being left alone.

When she was in her shirt, one of the men climbed the tree and brought her down to his king, who asked her many questions. She never answered, but the king was so taken by her beauty and grace that decided to marry her as soon as he could. The king's mother, however, did not like her at all, and reckoned she was unfit to be his son's spouse. When after a year, the young queen gave birth to the first child, her mother-in-law stole the baby while the queen slept and smeared her mouth with blood. Then, she accused the queen of having eaten her own child.

The king, her husband, did not believe it and protected his own queen, but when the same happened with the second and third child, the king had no choice but to let the justice run its course. The young queen was sentenced to be burnt at the stake as a witch.

The day she was to be executed, it also was the last day of the six years she had had to weave the shirts out of nettles, so that when she went to the stake, she fetched the six shirts she had woven. She surveyed the sky above her head. There was a strange, greyish atmosphere, full of anticipation, not unlike when a storm is about to start.

Suddenly, she saw the six swans flying towards her and before being tied at the stake, she threw the nettle shirts over them. They instantly turned into their handsome and strong brothers. Only the youngest had a swan wing instead of an arm because his sister had not been able to finish one of the sleeves of the shirt.

The brothers untied her and they all embraced and cried. The king was greatly moved at that sight. Then the young queen spoke for the first time in her own defence:

"Now my dear king and husband, I can talk and say how I was accused unjustly." And she told how her mother-in-law had plotted everything and had hidden their children. On hearing that, the king ordered his mother to bring back his children. When she had done so, he rejoiced in seeing that all of his children were safe and healthy. Then he had her tied and burnt at the stake for treason instead.

The king, the queen, their children and their six uncles lived in peace and abundance for many years to come.

Themes and Motifs

I have had a very close and personal interaction with this remarkable tale since I was a kid. I remember looking at a beautiful glossy illustration of the tale, featuring the heroine weaving shirts out of nettles, long before I could actually read the words. Even then, that image stayed with me and set in motion a peculiar sense of the mysterious and admiration for the heroine, who came across as a resilient, strong, young woman. An impression that was later confirmed through reading the tale. Indeed, seeing a young beautiful woman weaving nettles with her bare hands made me think of absolute, life-and-death need to do so, and I had faith in the heroine's motivations.

When I read the tale for the first time, I was enraptured and felt rewarded in discovering the heroine's motivation was brotherly love. I am an only child, yet some of my cousins were to me close to brothers, and I could relate to that kind of devotion. There are, however, other reasons why this tale has always fascinated me and I would discover them at each new reading.

I love the thoroughly wild setting of the tale. All the important events take place in the forest: the king goes out hunting and gets lost in the forest, thereby being forced to accept the hag's condition to get out. As a consequence, he marries a woman that makes the blood chill in his veins. He then has his children move into a castle in the forest to protect them. Yet, this is not enough and his wicked queen goes out into the forest and finds out their whereabouts. In the forest, she curses them into being swans. The little sister stays in the forest to escape from her stepmother and also comes to the thieves' den in the forest, where she speaks to her swan-brothers again. In the forest, she weaves shirts for them out of nettles, and there she is discovered by her future husband.

In the second part of the tale, after being convicted of infanticide and sentenced to death by fire, the forest is close by, or so I remember seeing in another glossy image of the same illustrated book, where the heroine was tied to the stake standing on a wooden platform in front of the castle, with the forest as a backdrop. Indeed, it seems to me that the forest is the more-than-human protagonist of this beautiful tale. It is the archetypal place of trial, mystery, and discovery, where much can be learned at the cost of great tests.

Certainly, there are interesting parallels between the forest, the king and the stepmother in the first part of the tale, and variations on the same elements in the second part: another forest, another king, another evil mother queen. The heroine has to face a similar set of circumstances twice, risking her own life, till she breaks the curse of the first queen, her stepmother.

As the latter had cursed the six children with silken shirts, so the heroine is to rescue them through shirts made of nettles, which of course is another significative symmetry in the structure of the tale.

On a psychological level, these recurring motifs bring home the intuitive truth that what we are not able to face and resolve comes back repeatedly in various forms in our lives, till we indeed solve the underlying issues.

The heroine can only break the curse by taking constant silent action: no words, no tears, no laughter, no songs, etc. She renounces to use her own voice to be able to save her own brothers. The final moment of acknowledgement and triumph, the anagnorisis, at the very end of the tale, is all the more powerful for it: "Now, dear king and husband, I can speak and say how I was accused unjustly"—she says in her true unwavering voice, speaking up for herself and receiving back all that she had lost: her sovereignty, brothers, children, husband, and kingdom.

This is yet another tale where the powerful use of silence and voice is a major theme. The way the heroine uses silence as a means of salvation and finally brings home her own vindication contains a remarkable lesson which could be summarised with the esoteric saying of many adepts: "To know, to dare, to will, to keep silent." Symbolically, the tale is much more than what meets the eye. It is about finding the place within where we can meet stillness and inner authority, where we anoint ourselves with the blessing of our higher—or deeper—selves.

As we saw in the previous chapter, birds are symbols of the soul, and swans are symbols of fierce beauty, grace, royalty, elegance, and the otherworldly dimension. The brothers can only exist as humans in the brief glow of the twilight, a liminal time when magic is afoot and the veil between the ordinary and the extraordinary is thin. With the knowledge she receives at this special time, the heroine dares to take action, to persevere in her will and to keep silent about it all, no matter what life throws at her. She takes in the good and the bad, and is strong enough to have a brush with death, risking to die at the stake, and yet not wavering.

As a reader, I love the perfect timing of the swan-brothers swooping down the wooden platform, being touched by the nettle shirts and turning into young men ready to free their sister. I love the fact that the heroine brings the shirts with her, her readiness even in the moment of her demise, how she scans the sky, trusting her brothers will come. And they do. The heroine is a cool-headed, resilient woman. Bringing the nettle shirts even in the direst moment points out her devotion to her brothers and also to her life work, which nobody can take away from her. What she has been working on in silence becomes the means of her liberation.

The message for the reader is not only one of resilience, but also of really valuing and treasuring our deepest work, talents, and gifts as marks of our individualities and of our destinies.

Another detail worth noticing is that the youngest brother keeps a wing instead of one of his arms because the sleeve of his shirt is unfinished. Our souls progress, transform and grow through life experiences that leave a mark. Something of what we went through stays with us, and it is up to us what we make of it, for good and for bad.

I like to imagine that the youngest brother is the favourite uncle of the heroine's children, who never tire of hearing the tale of when he wandered the skies as a swan. In other words, the teachings of times of trial do not go wasted if we allow them to become seeds that grow in the soul and can be shared with others too.

A swan wing is there to remind us of what we went through, what we learned, what we lost, what we value, lest we should forget. It is the feature that reminds us of who we have become. It can be compared to the archetypal wound of the wounded healer, which can never be healed. In fact, the wounded healer can only heal his or her community because of the wound that is the source of their power. The same applies to the swan wing. It is the mark of being close to the otherworldly and also the source of a peculiar, liminal status, whereby something of the swan-knowledge is retained by humans.

Swan-knowledge is mysterious soul knowledge, inspired knowledge, it is about grace earned at great cost: pain, loneliness, heaviness, sorrow, loss. Swan symbolism is also about inner beauty, trust and self-love: through their transformation into birds, the brothers and the heroine are changed and made stronger; that is, our whole psyche in all its aspects is transformed and integrated into a new configuration. In Psychosynthesis, it is remarked that there are many subpersonalities in the psyche of an individual. When they coexist quite harmoniously, our lives and psychological experiences are enhanced greatly. The reunion at the end of the tale is a great depiction of this outcome: the sister, the brothers, the king and the children are reunited and live in peace and abundance for many years.

Creative Process Activities

Activity n.1: Swan Journey

For the following activity, you will need a picture of one or more swans, such as a photograph or an image printed from the Web, music conveying a sense of the air element, a candle, your journal, and a pen. If you feel so inclined, do some research about swans' habits and characteristics as a preparation for your swan journey.

Put on comfortable, loose clothes. Sit or lie down on a mat and wrap yourself in a blanket. Make sure the room is darkened and you will be undisturbed for at least ten or twenty minutes.

Read aloud and record the following script that you will play to go on your journey into swan mode.

SCRIPT:

Relax. Breathe in and out, breathe in and out three times. Just be with your breath; do not alter the way you breathe. Breathe in and out three more times. In the darkness, close your eyes and feel the warm touch of the blanket on your arms, legs, hands, neck and cheeks. Imagine you are cocooned inside the wool; go deep within yourself, let go of all you did or you need to do later; just relax. Deeper and deeper. The blanket is a magical shell, a cocoon protecting you from the outside. Enjoy the warmth and soothing quality of the blanket. Remain in this silence and warmth for a while. PAUSE.

Now, feel the blanket turn into your second skin and envision swan plumage grow in the darkness all over your body, starting from your head and neck, down to your legs. Soon, your swan companions alight close to you, as you glide along a stream. You understand their language. Then, all together you spread your wide white wings and soar across the sky. You fly above countries, cities, seas and mountains, lakes and plains. You sense the winds and understand their directions. You let the wind make your flight full of ease and comfort. You are a swan. Your sight is sharp, your wings are strong, your whole body and neck are stretched out, feeling into the air like subtle receivers. You receive messages and inspirations from the clouds above, from lightning, and thunder, from the sun and the air spirits, the sylphs. PAUSE.

Listen to what these creatures have to say. Ask them for a personal message that may benefit you in your current circumstances or ask for a sign, a symbol. PAUSE.

Whatever you receive, thank the spirits and fly back across the sky into your body; feel the blanket become a simple blanket again, get in touch with the present moment, the darkness in your room, draw the blanket aside, open your eyes. Breathe. Now reach out for the candle and light it. Then, journal about your journey:

What did you feel, see, notice? Describe your sensations as a swan. What gift, symbol or sign did you receive from the air sprites? How can you apply their medicine to your life? Did they have a message for you? What was your takeaway? Over the next days, pay attention if and when a swan image or feather crosses your way. Be mindful.

Activity n.2: Swan Wing

Take an image of a swan wing and draw it on a large thick paper sheet. Decorate it with beads, ribbons, colours and gel pens, glitter or golden dust, or other objects. Add short phrases and single words that come to mind when you think of your swan journey. Then, cut out the swan wing. This is your swan wing, for you to keep as a reminder of the gifts you received and the discoveries you made as a swan. What characteristics of the swans could be useful to you? What attracts your curiosity regarding swans? What do they represent to you? Do some research and add a few facts in your wing space. Put your swan wing in a safe and handy place, and take it out every time you need a swan perspective.

Activity n.3: Voice Practice

For this activity, you only need yourself: your body, attention and breath. Sit comfortably on a chair, straightening your back, yet relaxing your muscles, shoulders, hands and jaws. Sit with your feet placed firmly on the ground and your legs and thighs slightly apart. Relax your hands, let your arms rest along your body and your hands be open and receptive.

Close your eyes and breathe from your abdomen: contract it as you inhale, hold and then relax it and exhale. Repeat the process a few times, till you feel relaxed and refreshed.

Next, pick a word. It can be a random word, or a word which is meaningful to you, that reminds you of something or resonates at this very time, or a word from the tale, such as "swan" or "forest". Experiment, try out all of these options and see what word sticks for you. Keep on breathing.

Then, intone the word you have chosen as a mantra. First, you will start in a low voice, and you will gradually increase the volume. Keep on breathing. Note where and when the sound you emit is free and easeful, and when it is constricted and difficult to make. Experiment with different melodies and intonations. Chant your mantra at least ten times. Pause and repeat the cycle at least three times.

Observe how your voice deepens, how your breath deepens, how your mind is relaxed, yet alert. If you are so inclined, repeat this voice practice every day. It only takes a few minutes. You can change the word, but experiment with the same mantra for at least a week. In this way, you are going to give yourself more time to dive into the characteristics and emotions evoked by the word, and to know more about the qualities you need at this time.

Enjoy the unfolding power and range of your voice, which will be more amplified as you practice. Finally, also notice how an ordinary word may take on a strange, numinous or unfamiliar quality as you repeat it again and again as a mantra, so that it may spark new ideas, insights and associations.

Conclusion

American writer and mythologist Joseph Campbell said that the journey of a lifetime is to become who we truly are. The protagonists of fairy and folk-tales testify to the adventures waiting on such a journey.

Joseph Campbell elaborated the idea of the hero's journey as a quest, while Maureen Murdock later distinguished the specifics of the heroine's journey as a fracture from the father's world, with both descending to the realm of the dark feminine, the suppressed aspects of the unconscious dimension. Despite their different ways of dealing with this dark dimension, both the hero and the heroine emerge from their quest changed and imbued with the 'elixir of life', which they share as a gift with their communities, on joining the world again.

On an individual level, all quests are quests for the wisdom of our bigger selves, engaging us in the process Carl G. Jung called individuation. Yet, as the tales point out, nobody can achieve individuation without going through certain stages, acknowledging them and being ready to take action in the world. Nobody can become individuated without engaging with the community, other humans and creatures, with the world and with nature, with the inner and outer dimensions of life.

Our journey together draws to a close for the time being, but you can engage with your favourite tales next. My suggestion is that you should re-read your favourite tales and keep a journal to record your ideas, memories, impressions, reactions and emotions. You may even write your own prequel or sequel to your favourite tales and interview the characters, or embody one of them through the writing of a first-person script and its dramatic enactment. The possibilities are endless. The goal is always, as in the Delphic motto, to "know thyself", and to know what is stirred up in the cauldron of your soul.

Essential Bibliography

Andersen, Hans C., 2013. *The Complete Fairy Tales and Stories*, Centaur Editions.

Calvino, Italo, (1956) 1980, 2000. *Italian Folk Tales*, translated by George Marin, Penguin.

Campbell, Joseph, (1949) 2020. *The Hero with a Thousand Faces*, third ed., Joseph Campbell Foundation.

Estés, Clarissa P., (1992) *Women Who Run with the Wolves*, Ballantine Books.

Franz, v. Marie L., (1970, 1973, 1996) 2017. *The Interpretation of Fairy Tales*, Shambhala Press.

Franz, v. Marie L., (1972, 1993) 2017. *The Feminine in Fairy Tales*, Shambhala Press.

Franz, v Marie L., (1977, 1990) 2017. *Individuation in Fairy Tales*, Shambhala Press.

Franz, v. Marie L., (1980) 2022. *Alchemy. An Introduction to the Symbolism and the Psychology*, Inner City Books.

Grimm, Jacob and Wilhelm, (1812) 2013. *The Complete Grimm's Fairy Tales*, illustrated by Arthur Rackham, Race Point Publishing.

Jacobs, Joseph, (1894) *English Fairy Tales.*

Jung, Carl. G., (1957-1979) *Collected Works*, Bollingen Series, Princeton University Press.

Jung, Carl. G., (1954) "Psychology of the Transference", in *Collected Works*, (Vol. 16).

Jung, Carl G., (1959, 1968) 1979 *The Archetypes and the Collective Unconscious* (CW, Vol. 9, Part I and II).

Jung, Carl G., (1961, 1962, 1963) 1989 *Memories, Dreams, Reflections*, recorded and edited by Aniela Jaffé, Random House, Vintage Books.

Jung, Carl G., 1995. *Jung on Active Imagination*, edited and with an introduction by Joan Chodorow, Princeton University Press.

Knightely, Thomas, (1882) *The Fairy Mythology.*

Murdock, Maureen, (1990) 2020 *The Heroine's Journey*, Shambhala Press.

Villeneuve, de Madame, (1740) *"Beauty and the Beast"*, abridged and rewritten in 1756 by Madame Leprince de Beaumont, retold in *The Blue Fairy Book* by Andrew Lang in 1889.

Beauty and the Beast. John D. Batten, 1916. Public domain.

www.ingramcontent.com/pod-product-compliance
Lightning Source LLC
Chambersburg PA
CBHW020906100426
42737CB00044B/498

* 9 7 8 1 7 3 7 0 5 4 5 9 7 *